Evan Thomas Radcliffe

a Cardiff Shipowning Company

Evan Thomas Radcliffe
a Cardiff Shipowning Company

by J. Geraint Jenkins

Amgueddfa Genedlaethol Cymru
National Museum of Wales
Cardiff 1982

Cover designed by Penknife
Typesetting by Characters
Printed by South Western Printers Ltd.
ISBN 0 7200 0247 8

Acknowledgements

Plate 1: Alun Davies; Plates 4, 12, 21: Edward Radcliffe Nelles; Plates 27, 28, 29: Aerofilms Ltd; Plates 10, 11, 13, 14, 15, 16, 17, 18: E. N. Taylor. The remainder are from the photographic archives of the Welsh Industrial and Maritime Museum, most of them from the Hansen Collection.

Preface

One of the more prosperous and best-known of Cardiff shipowning companies was that of Messrs. Evan Thomas, Radcliffe and Company, established in 1882 by a West Wales sea captain and a Merthyr Tudful businessman. Throughout its existence the company has always been based on Cardiff and many of its tramp steamers that sailed to all quarters of the globe were manned by Welsh seamen. Before 1939 the mainstay of the company's activities was the coal trade for during the last quarter of the nineteenth century and the first quarter of the twentieth century, vast quantities of Welsh steam coal were exported, the trade reaching its peak in the years immediately before the first World War.

J. Geraint Jenkins
Curator,
Welsh Industrial and Maritime Museum

The Coal Metropolis

In the 1880s, Cardiff was the boom-town of Victorian Britain, for as the result of the world-wide demand for Welsh steam coal to drive the ever-increasing number of steam ships, factories and railway locomotives, Cardiff, the natural gateway to the industrial valleys of Glamorgan and Gwent, developed into one of the great ports of Europe. Its trade was almost entirely tied up with the export of coal and in Butetown, the commercial heart of the town, new businesses were established by the dozen; fortunes were made and lost and Cardiff was a bustling, prosperous mecca that attracted thousands of immigrants from all parts of the world. In the early nineteenth century no one thought that the export of coal would ever play a significant part in the development of Cardiff for most of the trade of the new docks, when they were opened in 1839, was based almost entirely on the import of iron ore destined for the huge iron furnaces of Merthyr Tudful and the other ironworks located along the northern edge of the South Wales coalfield. Most of the exports were of iron products with a negligible amount of coal. In the narrow valleys of the coalfield itself, the coal seams were very deep and difficult to reach and the technology for extracting the coal was not available at the time. Nevertheless, by the 1860s, it had become possible to sink deep shafts and, as a result, there was a spectacular development in the coal mining industry in the South Wales valleys and areas like the Rhondda were transformed from rural backwaters into heavily industrialised conurbations. *From every part of Wales, the peasant trudges to the valleys among the Glamorgan and Monmouth hills or to the great seaports on the South Wales coast, all teeming with people. Coal, steel and tinplate, of world wide reputation have given energy to the labour, once bestowed indolently on peat and sheep and homespun.*[1] Cardiff was the natural gateway to the mineral wealth of the valleys and by the end of the nineteenth century, *the Severn sea is covered with ships carrying to all parts of the world the wealth of the inexhaustible mines in the mountains*[2] and Cardiff itself enjoyed such prosperity that it was referred to as *the coal metropolis of the world*.

In order to distribute the vast wealth of the coalfield to a world-wide market, a huge fleet of ships was necessary. Until the mid 1860s Cardiff had few ships of its own and most of the goods exported through the port were carried in vessels belonging to other ports, many of them foreign. The few ships owned by Cardiff men were engaged mainly in the coastal trade and most of the vessels were concerned with plying across the Bristol Channel to the creeks and harbours of the Somerset and Devon coast in small sailing vessels. In 1804 Cardiff had only 93 vessels with a total tonnage of 14,606 tons; an insignificant number when it is realised that in that year no fewer than 4,146 vessels were registered outwards from the port with cargoes destined for foreign ports and 7,768 vessels with coastwise cargoes.[3]

Cardiff Shipowners

The next two decades were to witness a spectacular increase in shipowning in Cardiff and iron vessels, driven by steam power, were purchased in great numbers by ambitious businessmen who set up operations in the heart of Butetown. Only a few of the old Cardiff sailing shipowners of earlier decades made the stride from sail to steam, for those that participated in the new boom came to Cardiff from elsewhere. For example, Philip and Thomas Morel and the Hacquoil Brothers came from the Channel Islands, John Cory came from Padstow in Cornwall, the Guerets came from France, the Turnbulls from Whitby in Yorkshire and the Gibbses from Portland. Some of the shipowners came from other parts of Wales; the Jenkins Brothers from Aber-porth in Dyfed, while J. Mathias of the Cambrian Steam Navigation Company had his offices at Baltic Chambers in his native Aberystwyth, as well as at Devon Buildings, James Street, Cardiff. Evan Thomas, too, was a native of Aber-porth, Dyfed and after serving as a master mariner with Jones Bros. of Newport and J. H. Anning of Cardiff, he went into partnership with Henry Radcliffe, a Merthyr Tudful businessman, and they purchased their first ship in 1881. The combination of master mariner on the one hand and businessman on the other was quite commonplace in Cardiff's dockland.

Evan Thomas and Henry Radcliffe

The village of Aber-porth on the shores of Cardigan Bay, some six miles north of the town of Cardigan, had a long history of maritime activity, for not only was it the most important centre of the herring fishing industry in Wales[4] but it also saw considerable commercial activity, especially in the mid nineteenth century. The south Cardiganshire coast is an area of high cliffs with deeply entrenched valleys and small villages nestling against the edge of the land. The isolation of the region meant that transport to this isolated, outer limb of Wales was always difficult in the past and the easiest way of importing the necessities of life was by sea. Aber-porth had its limekilns, warehouses and coal yards and a fleet of up to twenty vessels sailed from the village along the coasts of Wales, bringing in the essentials that the community could not produce itself. *The local ships, of 30 to 50 tons and manned by two men or two men and a boy, were owned by Aber-porth families. There were sixty-four shares in each ship but the usual unit of ownership was not one but four shares, that is a sixteenth part or as it was known "an ounce" of ship. At various times in the late nineteenth and early twentieth century, from fifteen to twenty such ships were owned by Aber-porth people, sometimes by groups of relatives, sometimes by companies of four or five people. At death they bequeathed their ounces and parts of ounces to others and this gave rise to complications of ownership.*[5] One family that was involved in shipowning at Aber-porth was that residing at Dolwen, a substantial house overlooking the beach. Hezekiah Thomas (1805 – 1869) was the owner of a vessel, the *Pheasant*, a ketch of 47 tons, and part-owner of a number of others. He was also concerned in the import and distribution of coal and limestone brought into Aber-porth by the coastal vessels from South Pembrokeshire and Carmarthen Bay. One son, Thomas Thomas (1836 – 1911), part-time sailor, part-time farmer, became secretary of the Aberporth Mutual Ship Insurance Society at a salary of £20 per annum in 1878 and his brother Evan (1832 – 1891), born and brought up in a village where seafaring was the main occupation, followed his father to sea. He obtained his master's certificate and after eight years as *Master in Steam in the tramps of the Baltic, Mediterranean, Black Sea, and United States of America* proposed the setting up of a new ship-owning company, not in his native Aber-porth which was, in any case, with the opening of the railway to Newcastle Emlyn and to Cardigan, declining very rapidly, but from Cardiff, the booming coal metropolis.[6] The vessel he purchased in association with Henry Radcliffe was delivered in March 1882 and went to sea under the command of Evan Thomas *a strong stalwart man with practical ability in navigation and all that implies.*

The other partner in the new venture was Henry Radcliffe, a native of Merthyr Tudful who was born in 1857 in that most important of Welsh industrial towns.

A trading smack and herring boats on the beach at Aber-porth, Ceredigion around 1890

Dôl-wen, Aber-porth. The birthplace of Capt. Evan Thomas

Henry Radcliffe 1855 – 1921

After receiving his education at Merthyr public school and grammar school . . . (he) *. . . obtained valuable commercial training with Messrs. Watts, Milburn & Company and Mr. J. H. Anning and gained experience which proved of the greatest value to him in after life.*[8] J. H. Anning, in particular, was an influential figure in Cardiff dockland for he was one of the few Cardiff shipowners who made the step from sail to steam with success. In 1876 he owned three sailing vessels[9] but by 1880 he owned three iron steamers.[10] Radcliffe, although only twenty-four years of age when he joined Evan Thomas in establishing the new shipping company, had already gained some experience in the business of chartering and shipowning. Nevertheless, it was in the name of Evan Thomas that a prospectus for the new company was launched in 1881.

Setting up the Company

Porthcawl, Bridgend
Glamorganshire
June 1881

Dear Sir,

I take the liberty of bringing under your notice a Steamer, for which I have contracted for, and shall be glad to know whether you are inclined to take an interest in the same.

The Steamer in question is to be built and engined by the well-known eminent firm of Messrs. PALMERS' SHIP BUILDING AND IRON CO., LIMITED, JARROW-ON-TYNE, to be classed 100 A1 at Lloyds, which is the highest class there is. Her dimensions are as follows:-

Length between perpendiculars..........225 feet
Breadth of Beam Moulded..........31 feet
Depth of Hold..........16 feet

Engines of 120 Horse-power; Cylinders, 28-inch and 52-inch, with 33-inch Stroke. She will carry about 1,500 tons on the light draught of 14 feet 10 inches water, and will be most suitable for the Bilbao Iron Ore Trade and the Grain Trade from the Danube, Nicolaieff, and the Azoff, where she can come from her loading berth to Sea with a full Cargo without incurring the enormous expense of lighterage and detention usually spent by Vessels of this tonnage both in the Danube and at Nicolaieff.

The price of this Steamer is £17,750. She will be divided into 64 Shares of £277 7s. per 64th Share, paid by easy instalments – one-third in Cash on delivery of Steamer, say March next; balance extending over a period of Two years.

I shall divide the profits at the end of each voyage, and will be the largest Shareholder in the Boat myself; and at the end of every Six months a printed Statement of Accounts will be issued to each of the Shareholders; the Books also will be open for inspection to any of the Shareholders during office hours at Cardiff.

My remuneration for the management of this Steamer is 2½ per cent on the gross earnings of the Boat; all brokerages, discounts, demurrages and earnings by the Ship will be credited to the benefit of the holders.

In case you are not acquainted with Shipping property, I may state that each Share is registered in the name of the Proprietor, at the Custom House, where the Steamer is registered by the Registrar of Shipping, which makes good the title which cannot possibly be tampered with.

Shares can be sold and transferred at any time the owner wishes, without any notice, in a few minutes, free of charge.

Of course the Steamer will be insured to her full value, and against every possible contingency, which makes Shipping Property as safe an investment as anything on dry land.

She will be completed and ready for Sea in March, next year.

A considerable number of the 64 Shares have already been taken up.

With every desire to avoid the least approach to exaggeration, I think I may safely say that you may rely on an annual return of from 20 to 24 per cent on this investment, even in the present depressed state of trade, and of course with a revival in trade the earnings will be considerably more.

I wish it to be clearly understood that I make no profit in any manner or shape upon the purchase and sale of this Steamer, but on the contrary, I offer the Shares to you at the net cost at which the same is built for me.

She will be fitted with Water Ballast, Donkey Boiler, and Steam Winches, Patent Windlass, and all other latest improvements for economy.

The experience that I have had for the past 8 years, as Master in Steam in the trades of the Baltic, Mediterranean, Black Sea, and United States of America, I think I may claim a very practical knowledge of Shipping and the trade in which I propose to work this Steamer, and I feel confidence in my ability to bring this experience to bear upon the undertaking to the profit of the Investors.

As references you can make your own enquiries about me or anyone here or in Cardiff.

Annexed is a form of Applications for Shares, which should be filled up and returned to the undersigned without delay.

Any further information you may require, I shall be glad to give you, by letter or personally.

Yours faithfully,
Evan Thomas

Form No. 10.

BILL OF SALE.

Official Number of Ship 78443 — Name of Ship Gwenllian Thomas

Port Number and Year of Registry 4/1882 — Port of Registry Swansea — British or Foreign built British — How propelled Screw Steam — Where built Jarrow — When built 1882

Number of Decks	One and a break	Build	Clencher	Length from forepart of Stem, under the bowsprit, to the aft side of the Head of the Stern-post	225 ft 4 tenths
Number of Masts	Two	Galleries	None	Mainbreadth to outside of Plank	31 ft 2 tenths
Rigged	Schooner	Head	None	Depth in Hold from Tonnage Deck to Ceiling at Midships	17
Stern	Elliptic	Framework	Iron	Depth in Hold from Upper Deck to Ceiling at Midships in the case of three Decks and upwards	—
				Length of Engine Room, if any	34 ft 7 tenths

	No. of Engines	Description	Whether British or Foreign made	When made	Name and Address of Makers	Diameter of Cylinders	Length of Stroke	No. of Horses' Power combined
Particulars of Engines, (if any)	Two	[illegible] surface condensing	British	1882	Palmers Ship Building and Iron Company Limited, Newcastle on Tyne	28 in / 52 in	33 in	99

Gross Tonnage	No. of Tons	Deductions Allowed	No. of Tons
Under Tonnage Deck	970·29	On account of Space required for Propelling Power	366·76
Closed-in Spaces above Tonnage Deck, if any, Space or Spaces between Deck		On account of Spaces occupied by Seamen or Apprentices, appropriated to their use, and kept free from Goods and Stores of every kind not being the personal property of the Crew. These Spaces are the following, viz.:	
Break	60·03	Lower Forecastle [illegible]	[illegible]
Bridge	69·67	Second Officer	[illegible]
Side houses	5·00	Second and third Engineers, First Officer, Mess room, First Engineer	21·70
Other closed-in Spaces, if any, as follows: [illegible]	2·24 / 10·88		
Gross Tonnage	1146·13	Total Deductions	414·24
Deductions as per Contra	414·24		
Registered Tonnage	731·89		

I Evan Thomas of Porthcawl in the County of Glamorgan Ship Owner in consideration of the sum of Two hundred & Eighty two pounds seventeen shillings & threepence paid to me by David Jones of Aberaman in the County of Glamorgan Licensed Victualler the Receipt whereof is hereby acknowledged, transfer One — Share in the Ship above particularly described, and in her boats, guns, ammunition, small arms, and appurtenances to the said David Jones

Further, I the said Evan Thomas for myself and my heirs, covenant with the said David Jones and his assigns, that I have power to transfer in manner aforesaid the premises herein-before expressed to be transferred, and that the same are free from incumbrances.

In witness whereof I have hereunto subscribed my name and affixed my seal this tenth day of January One thousand eight hundred and Eighty three

Executed by the above-named Evan Thomas in the presence of [illegible] Cardiff

Evan Thomas

Bill of Sale for the Gwenllian Thomas 1882

No difficulty at all was experienced in raising the necessary capital; most of it came from Wales.

Shareholder	Number of Shares
Evan Thomas and Hy Radcliffe (jointly)	1
Henry Anthony, Fleur de lis House, Newport Road, Cardiff	2
John Price, Palmer's Manager	2
Charles Jones, Newport Villa, Newport Road, Cardiff	2
Richard Holman, 23 St. Mary Avenue, London	1
John Holman & Sons, 23 St, Mary Avenue, London	1
Digery Gray, 3 Alford Place, Plymouth	2
John James, Ruabon	2
Rebecca Plummer, Rickard Arms, Treforest	2
Charles Roberts, Glyndwr Terrace, Corwen	1
Robert Ferdinand Graisser, Argoed Hall, Ruabon	2
Henry Evans, Ivy House, Tongwynlais, Cardiff	2
F. W. Baddeley, Hotwell Villa, Brixham, Devon	2
Jane Roberts, Union Terrace, Corwen	1
Jenkin David, N. P. Bank Ltd., Dolgelly	1
Thos. Henry, Newport Villa, Newport Road, Cardiff	1
Arthur Ll. Hopkins, 19 The Walk, Cardiff	1
Anthony Appleton, 2 School Terrace, Corwen	1
Frederick Jones, 19 High Street, Ilfracombe	1
Rev. J. Cynddylan Jones, 2 Richmond Crescent, Cardiff	1
Wm. Howell, Farmer, Pencoed, Bridgend	1
David Guy, Bute Street, Cardiff	1
Rev. Wm. James, Conway Road, Cardiff	1
Jenkin Henry, Newton Nottage, Nr. Bridgend	1
Capt. H. Dolton, 23 Northcote Street, Cardiff	1
Elizabeth Evans, 18 Sapphire Street, Cardiff	1
John Price, Laurel Cottage, Pencoed, Bridgend	1
Richard Diggory, 2 Glyndwr Terrace, Corwen	1
Elizabeth Maria Edwards, 2 Woodfield Place, Cardiff	1
Thomas Davies, 13 South Luton Place, Cardiff	1
Salvatore Camillieri, Official General Post Office, Valletta, Malta	1
David Davies, Pier Head House, Bute Dock, Cardiff	1
Dr. J. E. Jones, Brynffynnon, Dolgelly	1
Dominic Framontana, Ship Agent, Palermo	1
John Miller, Patrick Street Grocer, Cardiff	1
John Jacob Davies, 4 South Church Street, Cardiff	1
Evan David, Shipowner, Porthcawl, Glam.	1
Samuel Greck, Valletta, Malta	1
David Rowlands, 80 High Street, Bala	1
Kate Dart, 2 Manor Terrace, Brixham	1
Mary Dart, 2 Manor Terrace, Brixham	1
Lewis Thomas, 25 Park Place, Cardiff	1
J. Carew, Grocer, South Luton Place, Cardiff	1
Thomas & Henry Watkins (jointly), Victoria Inn, Porthcawl	1
David Jones, Victoria House, Aberavon, Glam.	1

Thomas Tyler (Capt.), 12 Granville Street, Hull	1
James Gregg, Springfield, Dolgelly	1
Thomas Thomas & Sisters (jointly), Dolwen, Aberporth, Cardigan	1
Joseph Wheeler, 90 Clifton Street, Cardiff	1
Wm. Jones, 3 Wharf Street, Cardiff	1
Hy. John, 3 Wharf Street, Cardiff	1
John H. Birmingham, Mynde Park, Hereford	1
Wm. Davies, Grocer, 145 Clifton Street, Cardiff	1

Evan Thomas and Henry Radcliffe, like most other shipowners of the period, risked very little of their own money in the new venture. *It was a relatively easy matter to set up as a shipowner,* says Daunton,[11] . . . *ships were bought on mortgage. The capital was realised by shares in single-ship companies, which were partly bought by tradesmen who would expect orders in return, but were otherwise largely sold outside South Wales. The person who really profited was the manager of the company, the person who had floated it. He took a commission on gross earnings rather than profits so that, provided he was getting a freight he was not concerned with the profitability of the company. . . But leaving aside possible abuses the system of single-ship companies did permit newcomers (scrupulous and unscrupulous) to enter the industry. The system could permit rapid growth and high dividends and not merely exploit the shareholders.* The development of steamships especially built for the coal trade and the ease of raising capital gave newcomers like Thomas and Radcliffe a chance to enter business without having to write off capital. This was one reason why many of the shipowners of an earlier era failed in their attempt to transfer from sail to steam. With single-ship companies the practice was of advantage in that the liability of a company was limited to the value of one ship and although in 1894 the Merchant Shipping Act limited liability to specific figures it was still an advantage to set up one-ship companies especially when dealing with jurisdiction in some foreign courts.

The Early Years

As Evan Thomas Radcliffe's business succeeded, more and more ships were added to the fleet. As many as 31 single-ship companies were registered in the company's name.

Companies	Registered
Anne Thomas S.S. Co.	14 July, 1883
Clarissa Radcliffe S.S. Co.	10 April, 1888
Picton S.S. Co.	15 November, 1925
Gwenllian Thomas S.S. Co.	28 July, 1894
Clarissa Radcliffe S.S. Co.	18 June, 1904
Llangorse S.S. Co.	13 January, 1899
W.I. Radcliffe S.S. Co.	5 February, 1886
Wynnstay S.S. Co.	1 October, 1883
Wimborne S.S. Co.	10 June, 1899
Colonies S.S. Co.	4 April, 1908
Patagonia S.S. Co.	15 November, 1905
Llanishen S.S. Co.	26 November, 1909
Llanover S.S. Co.	24 December, 1908
Swindon S.S. Co.	6 July, 1898
Euston S.S. Co.	16 May, 1898
Paddington S.S. Co.	14 February, 1898
Llandudno S.S. Co.	20 November, 1896
Windsor S.S. Co.	2 November, 1896
Kate Thomas S.S. Co.	1 October, 1893
Sarah Radcliffe S.S. Co.	10 October, 1888
Bala S.S. Co.	27 February, 1884
Walter Thomas S.S. Co.	5 October, 1883
Mary Thomas S.S. Co.	13 November, 1888
Jane Radcliffe S.S. Co.	23 May, 1889
Douglas Hill S.S. Co.	28 October, 1889
Manchester S.S. Co.	15 March, 1890
Iolo Morgannwg S.S. Co.	17 November, 1882
Dunraven S.S. Co.	31 March, 1894
Anthony Radcliffe S.S. Co.	date not known
Ethel Radcliffe S.S. Co.	date not known

The new shipping company must have succeeded beyond the owners' dreams. The *Gwenllian Thomas* went to sea under the command of Evan Thomas, his partner taking charge of the office at 4 Dock Chambers and all the chartering arrangements. In 1882, a second vessel, the *Iolo Morgannwg* (1,292 tons) was purchased from Palmers of Newcastle who had already built the *Gwenllian Thomas.* In 1883 came the *Kate Thomas* (1,588 tons) and the *Anne Thomas* (1,419 tons) followed by the *Wynnstay* (1,542 tons) in 1884. Around this time Evan Thomas gave up the sea, but he had the satisfaction to know that when he

Gwenllian Thomas 1882

died on the 14 November, 1891 the company he had established less than ten years previously owned as many as 15 tramp steamers. Evan Thomas left a son and four daughters.

With the death of Evan Thomas in 1891 at the age of 49, the business was expanding at such a rate that Henry Radcliffe took into partnership, his younger brother Daniel who, from 1892 when he joined the firm until his death in 1933, was one of the most influential men in Cardiff dockland. With eight years' experience with Cardiff shipowners J. H. Anning and the Turnbull Brothers, Daniel Radcliffe, at the age of twenty four, promoted the rapid growth of the company with the result that in 1900, the firm owned a total of 24 ships.[12]

Most of the early vessels were equipped with sails as well as engines; for example, the *Gwenllian Thomas* was a steamer but it was also equipped with sails. In the Bill of Sale, she was classified as *a two-masted, schooner-rigged vessel* equipped with *two inverted direct-acting compound surface condensing engines* producing '99 *horses power.* The vessel measured 225 feet long, 31.2 feet wide and had a draught of 17 feet. She was built and engined by Palmer's Shipbuilding and Iron Company of Jarrow-on-Tyne. Her gross tonnage was 1146.13 tons and the vessel was typical in size and design to many of the vessels purchased by the dozen by Cardiff shipowners during the last two decades of the nineteenth century. After trials the vessel arrived in Cardiff on the 24 June, 1882 and left on her maiden voyage with 1,457 tons of steam coal for St. Nazaire at a freight rate of

Daniel Radcliffe 1860 – 1933

£341-0s-5d. From St. Nazaire the vessel sailed in ballast for Bilbao in northern Spain, returning to Cardiff's Roath Dock with a cargo of iron ore. She continued in this trade from Cardiff – St. Nazairae – Bilbao – Cardiff and then undertook three voyages from Cardiff to Gibraltar, returning each time to Liverpool with copper ore from Huelva. For most of her working life, the *Gwenllian Thomas* was mainly concerned with carrying coal to continental and Mediterranean ports, with occasional voyages to the Black Sea and the Sea of Azov, returning to Britain with loads of grain. She made a gross profit of £34,008 for the company and when she was sold to Richard Selmer, a Norwegian shipowner in December 1905, Evan Thomas Radcliffe still obtained £8775-13s-3d for her. The vessel was finally sunk after a collision on 1 November, 1910.

Investment in the various single-ship companies owned by Evan Thomas Radcliffe during the first two decades of its existence were heavy. New ships were expensive and much capital was necessary to purchase them. The following were prices paid to the builders of some of the earlier ships.

Gwenllian Thomas (1882)	£17,000
Llanberis (1896)	£34,000
W. I. Radcliffe (1896)	£45,788
Washington (1893)	£52,392
Wimborne (1898)	£35,566
Llangorse (1900)	£45,144
Llangollen (1900)	£49,371

Anne Thomas 1882

Much of the investment in the companies came from rural Wales, and it is surprising that big business concerns are hardly represented in the list of investors. The Anne Thomas S.S. Co., when it was formed in 1883, for example, attracted shareholders, each one purchasing a £100 share, from North Wales – especially from the towns and villages of Dolgellau, Ruthin, Betws-y-Coed, Bala and Corwen. They included Jenkin David, Evan Thomas's brother-in-law who was a bank manager at Dolgellau, and a number of farmers, schoolmasters, quarrymen, railway workers, woollen manufacturers and Methodist ministers who were possibly customers of Jenkin David's bank. Shareholders included Thomas Gee, the well-known Denbigh publisher, and one of the most famous and renowned preachers of his time, the Rev. J. Cynddylan Jones. Members of the Thomas family who still resided at Dolwen, Aber-porth each possessed a share as did members of the Radcliffe family.

In the early years of the company, vessels were always purchased from shipbuilders in the north-east of England and each vessel was designed to the company's specifications. Palmers of Jarrow built most of the vessels constructed in the 1880s, the exception being one vessel – the *Bala* of 1884, which was built by William Gray & Co, of West Hartlepool. In the 1890s, with the control of the company passing into the hands of the Radcliffe family, Ropner's of Stockton-on-Tees became the main supplier of vessels during the earlier part of the decade. Ropner's had considerable connection with Cardiff, for a number of local shipowners – W. J. Tatem, J. E. Morel, W. Leon and William Seager – were all directors of the Ropner Shipbuilding and Repair Company. One vessel, the *Peterston* of 1892 was built by Thomas Turnbull of the Whitehall Dockyard in Whitby.

Jane Radcliffe 1890

Llanberis 1890

W. I. Radcliffe 1896

Daniel Radcliffe had received his early business training with the Turnbull Brothers who had established a shipowning business in Cardiff and it was perhaps only natural that when Daniel went into business with his brother Henry in 1892 that he should have ordered his first ship from Thomas Turnbull. By the late 1890s Richardson Duck & Co. of Thornaby-on-Tees were the main suppliers of considerably larger vessels, for few of those built after 1885 were less than 3,000 gross registered tons, while many of those built after 1903 were well over 4,500 gross tons; the sister ships *Picton* and *Patagonia* of 1906 being over 5,000 tons. The boom years 1910 to 1914 saw the purchase of three even larger vessels of over 6,000 tons – the *Wimborne* and *Windsor* of 1911 and the *Patagonia* of 1913, all purchased from Craig, Taylor & Co., Stockton-on-Tees.

Many of the vessels built in the early years of the company's activities were named after members of the owners' families. For example, Kate, Anne and Gwenllian Thomas were Evan Thomas's daughters, Walter his only son and Mary his sister. W. I. Radcliffe (Wyndham Ivor Radcliffe) was Henry's only son and Clarissa his daughter. The prefix '*Llan*' which was to characterise Radcliffe's ships in the inter-war period made an appearance with the launching of the *Llanberis* in 1890.

Wyndham Ivor Radcliffe: Henry Radcliffe's only son

BUILDERS OF RADCLIFFE VESSELS 1882–1917

Builder	1882–1890	1891–1900	1901–1910	1911–1915
Palmers Shipbuilding & Iron Co., Jarrow-on-Tyne	*Gwenllian Thomas* *Anne Thomas* *Iolo Morgannwg* *Kate Thomas* *Walter Thomas* *Wynnstay* *W. I. Radcliffe* *Mary Thomas* *Clarissa Radcliffe* *Douglas Hill*	*Anthony Radcliffe*		
Ropner Shipbuilding & Repair Co., Stockton-on-Tees	*Sarah Radcliffe* *Jane Radcliffe* *Llanberis*	*Dunraven* *Llandudno* *Windsor* *Euston* *Paddington*	*Clarissa Radcliffe*	
John Blumer & Co., North Dock, Sunderland			*Boverton* *Euston*	
Tyne Iron Shipbuilding Co., Willington Quay-on-Tyne			*Dunraven* *Llandudno*	
Wm. Gray & Co., West Hartlepool	*Bala* *Manchester*			
Thomas Turnbull, Whitehall Dockyard, Whitby		*Peterston*		
Craig, Taylor & Co., Stockton-on-Tees				*Wimborne* *Windsor* *Patagonia* *Penistone* *Flimston* *Clarissa Radcliffe* *W. I. Radcliffe*
Irvine & Co., West Hartlepool		*Ethel Radcliffe*		

Builder	1882–1890	1891–1900	1901–1910	1911–1915
Richardson, Duck & Co, Thornaby-on-Tees		*Wimborne* *Swindon* *Llanover* *Llandrindod* *Llangollen* *Llangorse*	*Llanishen* *W. I. Radcliffe* *Patagonia* *Picton* *Washington*	
Joseph L. Thompson & Sons, Sunderland			*Hanley* *Gwent*	
A. Rodger & Co., Port Glasgow			*Aden* (ex *Craigmore*)	

The Black Sea Trade

All the Radcliffe vessels were tramp steamers, sailing not along fixed routes but to whatever port in the world the charterers wished. Nevertheless, from 1882 when the company was established until about 1914 there was a pattern of trading with the vessels taking out cargoes of coal from the Tyne ports and South Wales to west European or Mediterranean ports, then proceeding in ballast to the Black Sea, to such ports as Odessa, Taganrog and Novorossisk, returning to a British, but more likely a continental port, with grain. This became so much the normal pattern of trading that the annual reports of the company constantly refer to the Black Sea traffic. For example the *Washington* in 1907 *is now unloading at Port Said and will probably proceed to the Black Sea to load for home.* In 1911 *owing to the down tools strike the vessel was obliged to proceed to the Black Sea in ballast and she is now loading at Nicolaieff for Hamburg;* or in 1912 *owing to the great coal strike we were unable to get any outward cargo and had to bunker the steamer on the Continent at famine prices to enable us to proceed in ballast to the Black Sea to load for home.*

The following are some examples of the trading pattern of some of the Radcliffe ships during the first decade of the present century.

S.S. Llangorse

1907	Sept. 30	Barry – Port Said – coal
	Nov. 7	Odessa – Kherson – Rotterdam – grain (barley, rye, maize)
1908	Jan. 8	Cardiff – Port Said – coal
	March 6	Barry – Port Said – coal
	May 4	Odessa – Antwerp – grain
	June 18	Cardiff – Venice – coal
	Oct. 3	Nicolaieff & Odessa – Rotterdam – grain
	Nov. 11	Barry – Port Said – coal
1909	Jan. 7	Novorossisk – Rotterdam – grain
	Feb. 3	Cardiff – Ancona – coal
	April 24	Nicolaieff – Hamburg – grain
	June 4	Barry – Port Said – coal

S.S. Patagonia

1906	July 11	Cardiff – Ancona – coal
	Sept. 1	Odessa – Rotterdam – grain
	Oct. 6	Barry – Port Said – coal
	Nov. 19	Odessa – Hamburg – grain
1907	Jan. 10	Cardiff – Port Said – coal
	Feb. 29	Theodosia & Novorossisk – Hamburg – grain

April 13	Barry – Port Said – coal
June 11	Nicolaieff – Odessa – Hamburg – grain
July 19	Barry – Port Said – coal
Sept. 5	Odessa – Rotterdam – grain
Oct. 26	Barry – Trieste – coal
Dec. 19	Barry – Port Said – coal

This pattern of trading was repeated for almost all the Radcliffe ships with little variation until 1912 – 13 when there was a decline in the trade. *The freights homeward from the Black Sea have now fallen off considerably from the high point they used to be* said the company's annual report for 1912. Gradually the Black Sea trade declined and Evan Thomas Radcliffe, in common with other Cardiff shipowners, had to look elsewhere for their trade. The Black Sea trade in its heyday was a very lucrative business and the carriage of coal from South Wales outwards and grain from southern Russia inwards really provided the basis of success for Radcliffes. Vessels rarely sailed in ballast except for short voyages from the points of discharge of coal to the Black Sea and from continental ports to Cardiff or Barry. The following gross earnings were obtained by some of the vessels in the period before 1914.

S.S. Gwenllian Thomas	June 1882 – December 1905	£34,008-0s-3d
S.S. Gwent	April 1909 – April 1912	£13,365-0s-7d
S.S. Anne Thomas	September 1883 – January 1912	£31,814-18s
S.S. Badminton	January 1910 – February 1912	£5,469-15s-7d
S.S. Llanberis	February 1890 – March 1910	£46,891-8s-8d
S.S. Wynnstay	March 1884 – October 1904	£41,771-6s-8d
S.S. W.I. Radcliffe	July 1886 – October 1904	£48,024-14s-6d
S.S. Anthony Radcliffe	September 1893 – Feb. 1908	£46,651-18s-9d
S.S. Ethel Radcliffe	November 1894 – Dec. 1907	£45,144-7s-5d
S.S. Wimborne	Dec. 1898 – Nov. 1910	£51,421-11s-9d
S.S. Boverton	Sept. 1910 – March 1912	£5,806-14s-10d
S.S. Clarissa Radcliffe	Oct. 1904 – April 1913	£46,132-7s-9d

In communicating with the shareholders of the various single ship companies the following circular letter of 1912 is typical of the optimism expressed by the directors at a period when the Cardiff tramp steamer trade was at its height:

The Wimborne Steamship Company Limited

4, Dock Chambers
Cardiff, July 11th 1912

Ladies and Gentlemen,

We have pleasure in handing you annexed Account of the working of this Company from November 4th last to June 13th, duly audited. On March 9th you had a dividend of £3 per Share, and we now have pleasure in handing you a further £2 per each £100 Share, free of Income Tax, as interim dividend making in all £5 per Share for the period covered. Kindly acknowledge receipt of enclosed cheque and oblige.

We now have pleasure in informing you that some time ago we disposed of the BOVERTON and replaced her by a new steamer named WIMBORNE, which was guaranteed to carry 9,500 tons (but carries considerably more). She was contracted for at the lowest period in prices, but including our specification (with all its extras), which is many thousands of pounds in excess of what is necessary to secure the highest class at Lloyds, and we dare say Builders would ask at least £10,000, if not more today to repeat the Contract, with delivery not before 12 months hence, so therefore as a Commercial entity we should judge that the Steamer is worth about £15,000 more than her contract. Particulars of the above transaction will appear in the Annual Accounts as usual. The Steamer was built by Messrs. Craig, Taylor & Co., and engined by Messrs. Blair, both of Stockton-on-Tees, and she is, in our opinion, one of the most magnificent cargo Steamers that has ever been built, embracing the whole of our extras. At the time she went to sea the ''Wimborne'' Company was £11,495 short of the amount necessary to complete the purchase, and this amount we arranged to advance at the low rate of 4% per annum interest. In the meantime, she has been able to pay off £4,500, thus leaving only £6,995 to be dealt with in the future besides sending you £5 per each £100 Share in about 7 months, and if freights maintain their recent firmness, and we are not entrammelled by these continual dreaded Strikes, we do not see any difficulty in paying this balance off out of earnings in a very short time, in addition to distributing satisfactory dividends.

You will remember that the original WIMBORNE carried 5,850 tons, whereas the present vessel carries nearly 4,000 tons more, and being new has at least 20 years first-class trading ahead. With this dividend, you have now received £123.2.6 for each £100 invested, and the earnings of the Company up to the present, covering a period of about 13½ years amount to £60,400 which is £25,400 in excess of the original Capital. Many of the Shareholders will know that several Shipping Companies inaugurated since this one have come to grief, whilst others have been reconstructed by reducing their Capital to half, and some even more, and we venture to say that if the Directors of those Companies could have exercised the same ability, foresight, and careful financing that we have done in the case of this company, their Capital would not only have been saved but greatly enhanced, as is the case with this company. We think we can fairly ask, what outside Shipping Companies can produce such a magnificent result as this?

Our Commodore Master, the late Capt. E. H. Dolton, who had been associated with us from the commencement, namely 30 years ago, took command of the WIMBORNE on her first voyage, and in his letter dated the 12th December last, he made the following remark:-

''The WIMBORNE is very much admired by all, and in my opinion she ''is the most up-to-date cargo Steamer afloat; I trust to have great success ''with her''.

We had great respect for his opinion, as he was no ordinary Shipmaster; indeed, we question whether the British Nation has produced a better man. As you already know he died suddenly at Norfolk (Virginia, U.S.A.) while the

WIMBORNE called there for Coal, and his body was brought home in his own Ship to be buried in his native town of Brixham, and he was laid to rest amidst the respect and deep regret of all his friends. We are sure you will share our sorrow and that of the widow and family at the sad loss that has befallen them and ourselves.

The Steamer is now on passage to Venice. She has a fair outward rate, but the homeward freights from the Black Sea have for the present fallen off somewhat, but we expect that by the time the WIMBORNE is ready to load home the homeward market may have improved, as by then the new grain should be arriving at the different shipping ports.

We are, Ladies and Gentlemen,
Yours faithfully,
Evan Thomas Radcliffe & Co.

P.S. – We have just received a communication from a London Steamship Company in which we are interested. Thirteen years ago, we invested £500 in this Company, and during that time we have had £210 in dividends, the Steamer has been sold, and after paying her debts, &c., there is now only £12.17.0 per Share coming to the Shareholders, or a total of £64.5.0 upon our investment of £500. This is typical of many, (and some are even worse), of our investments in Shipping Companies under other managements.

The Black Sea trade did continue until the early years of the first World War, but some of the vessels were making more frequent appearances in America and south east Asia. For example, the *S.S. Washington*, from its building in 1907 until December 1912, was concerned exclusively with the carriage of coal from South Wales to the Mediterranean and the carriage of grain from the Black Sea ports to Hamburg, Rotterdam and Marseilles. In December 1912 she sailed from Barry with a cargo of coal from Rio de Janeiro. She then returned from Bahia Blanca to London with grain and left on another voyage from Barry to Rio de Janeiro returning to Rotterdam with general cargo from New Orleans. She then returned to the Black Sea trade for another five voyages before sailing in ballast after unloading coal at Taranto for Pondicherry, returning with a cargo of ground nuts for Marseilles. She then sailed across the Atlantic to New Orleans returning to Marseilles in February 1914 with a cargo of wheat. The *S.S. Llangorse*, to quote another example, was used exclusively for the normal Black Sea coal and grain trade from 1907 to 1912; she then crossed the Atlantic to Baltimore returning to Hamburg with grain. After six more voyages to the Black Sea the vessel visited Galveston, La Plata, Buenos Aires, Philadelphia, Rosario, San Nicholas and Aguilas being concerned with the transport of grain and iron ore, to Naples, Barcelona, Glasgow, Genoa and Avonmouth. Gradually, the trans-Atlantic trade was becoming more and more important in the activities of Cardiff shipowners.

Iolo 1898

Bonvilston 1903

Aden 1905

Boverton 1910

Euston 1910

W. I. Radcliffe 1913

The 1914 – 18 War

At the outbreak of war in 1914, Messrs. Evan Thomas Radcliffe were the largest of the Cardiff shipowners owning a fleet of 28 vessels. They were:

Ship	Built	Gross Registered Tons
Bala	1894	2874
Dunraven	1910	3117
Euston	1910	2841
Jane Radcliffe	1897	4074
Llanberis	1897	4064
Llandrindod	1900	3841
Llandudno	1910	4187
Llangollen	1900	3842
Llangorse	1900	3941
Llanishen	1901	3837
Patagonia	1913	6011
Picton	1906	5083
Sarah Radcliffe	1896	3333
Swindon	1906	5084
W. I. Radcliffe	1904	4749
Washington	1907	5080
Wimborne	1911	6079
Windsor	1912	6055
Gileston	1898	2728
Clarissa Radcliffe	1913	6042
Llanover	1904	4703
Aden	1905	2426
Bonvilston	1893	2866
Boverton	1910	2958
Iolo	1898	3903
Paddington	1859	3840
Gwent	1901	3344
Badminton	1899	3847

During the first World War the company was to suffer considerable losses, a total of 20 ships being sunk. They were:

Bonvilston (1908) ex *Anthony Radcliffe* (1893). Torpedoed 17th October 1918 9½ miles N.W. by W of Corsedale Point.

Sarah Radcliffe (1896) sunk by submarine 170 miles S.W. of Ushant

Jane Radcliffe (1911) ex *Windsor* (1897) Torpedoed 28 November 1917 2 miles SW of Antimilo, Greek Archipelago.

Iolo (1913) ex *Paddington* (1898) sunk by submarine 11 October 1916 153 miles N. of Vardo, Norway.

Swindon (1899) sunk by submarine gunfire 23 July 1916 63 miles NE by N of Cape Carson, Algeria.

Iolo (1917) ex *Llanover* (1899). Torpedoed 17 February 1917, 42 miles SW of Fastnet.

Llandrindod (1900). Torpedoed 18 May 1917 165 miles NW by W of Fastnet.

Llangorse (1900). Torpedoed 48 miles WSW of Cape Matapan.

Llanishen (1901). Torpedoed and beached 9th August 1917, 8 miles N by E of Cape de Crews, Gulf of Lyons.

Llancarfan (1917) ex *W. I. Radcliffe.* Torpedoed 16th May 1918 370 miles E by N from San Miguel, Azores.

Paddington (1917) ex *Patagonia* (1906). Torpedoed 21 July 1917 250 miles W of Fastnet.

Washington (1917). Torpedoed 3 May 1917 in Rapallo Bay off Genoa.

Dunraven (1910) 10 August 1917. Torpedoed in Bay of Biscay.

Euston (1910). Torpedoed 25 October 1917 35 miles SW of Cape Matapan.

Llandudno (1910) 1 August 1917. Captured and sunk by submarine 110 miles SW of Porqueolles Island, Gulf of Lyons.

Windsor (1911). Sunk by submarine gunfire 21 October 1915. 70 miles SW of Lizard.

Patagonia (1913). Torpedoed 15 September 1915 10½ miles NE of Odessa.

Penistone (1913). Torpedoed 11 October 1918 145 miles SW by S of Nantucket.

Flimston (1915). Captured and sunk by submarine 18 December 1916 21 miles NE by E of Ushant.

Post-War Depression

Although substantial sums of money were received in compensation for the vessels lost during the war, Radcliffes, unlike some other Cardiff shipowning companies, did not immediately enter the post-war market for very expensive ships and only one vessel, the *Ethel Radcliffe*, was purchased in 1920 as a replacement for the 20 vessels lost in the war. In 1919, the company owned nine vessels only, with a total gross tonnage of 41,254. The ships were:

Boverton (b. 1910	2959 gross tons
Clarissa Radcliffe (b. 1915)	5754 gross tons
Gileston (b. 1898)	2728 gross tons
Llanberis (b. 1897)	4064 gross tons
Llangollen (b. 1900)	3842 gross tons
Llangorse (b. 1904)	4703 gross tons
Picton (b. 1906)	5083 gross tons
W. I. Radcliffe (b. 1913)	6042 gross tons
Wimborne (b. 1911)	6078 gross tons

Obviously the real boom in the fortunes of the Bute Docks in Cardiff was the period immediately before the first World War when incredible quantities of Welsh coal were exported in Welsh ships to all quarters of the globe. The war marked a turning point in the fortunes of South Wales, for between 1914 and 1918, the markets for Welsh coal were restricted and many were closed. It meant that many a country which had been dependent on Welsh coal, developed their own energy resources during a period when Welsh coal was not available to them. When the war ended it became almost impossible to regain a foothold in a market that had been virtually closed for four years and where in the meantime home production of coal had largely replaced imports. Coal was being used more economically as the result of improvements in boiler and furnace techniques; the internal combustion engine was revolutionising internal transport with serious consequences for the railways and perhaps more importantly for South Wales, oil was replacing coal in steam ships and motor ships replacing steam ships.[13] Voyages by Radcliffe ships to such coaling ports as Port Said, Alexandria and Malta regularly undertaken before 1914 became far less regular. In the post-1918 period far too much coal was being produced throughout the world and consequently Welsh coal was not in world-wide demand as it was a few years earlier. Consequently there was a sharp decline in the fortunes of the export-orientated South Wales ports.

Nevertheless, the immediate post-war period was marked by a terrific growth in shipowning in Cardiff, as many shipowners attempted to replace the heavy losses sustained during the war. Old established companies as well as a number of newcomers to the industry began to purchase vessels at greatly inflated prices during a period that soon proved to be a false dawn. *After the war* says Chappell[14] *ship-owning at Cardiff developed from a business to a craze. The Port became the centre of a great shipping boom, which attracted millions of pounds from investors and speculators in all parts of the United Kingdom. From 1918 onwards, for several years, phenomenal activity was in the formation of new shipping companies and ships were purchased at fabulous prices. . . The boom did not however, last long. In 1920, there came a sudden and catastrophic reduction of freights by amounts ranging in some cases from 50 to 300 per cent. The inflated shipping values shrunk in unison, many of the companies got into financial difficulties and had to be wound up, and their tonnage was sold at sums enormously below cost.* Luckily for Evan Thomas Radcliffe, no attempt was made in 1918 and 1919 to purchase extra ships, so that the company, unlike some others in Cardiff was well able to weather the storm of the slump of the 1920s. The one new vessel, the *Ethel Radcliffe*, of 5,673 gross tons was built for the company by Craig Taylor & Co. of Stockton-on-Tees at a greatly inflated cost of £274,019 and she sailed on her maiden voyage under the command of Capt. M. Mathias of Cardigan with a cargo of coal for Port Said; she then sailed in ballast to Mauritius returning to London with a cargo of sugar, then to Norfolk, Virginia in ballast to return to Immingham with a cargo of coal. The pattern of trading for all ships had obviously changed from pre-1914 days. The following are examples of voyages undertaken by some Radcliffe ships in 1919 – 20:

S.S. Boverton

May 17	1919	Cardiff – Malta – coal.
July 10	1919	Ingramport – Manchester – coal.
August 25	1919	Penarth – Leghorn – coal.
September 23	1919	Sfax – Plymouth – phosphates.
November 8	1919	Barry – Naples – coal.
January 8	1920	Plate – Hull – linseed and maize.
March 6	1920	Tyne – London – coal.
April 1	1920	Newport – Liverpool – coal.
April 24	1920	Cardiff – Liverpool – coal.
May 8	1920	Barry – Liverpool – coal.
May 20	1920	Newport – Naples – coal.
June 25	1920	Bougie – Middlesborough – iron ore.
July 27	1920	Barry – Buenos Aires – in ballast.
September 7	1920	Rosario – Tralee – maize.
November 18	1920	Barry – Marseilles – coal.
December 17	1920	Carthagena – West Hartlepool – iron ore.

S.S. Wimborne

May 1	1919	Newport – Alexandria – coal.
July 10	1919	Rangoon – Liverpool – rice.
October 28	1919	Liverpool – Sydney C.B. – in ballast.
November 23	1919	St. Johns N.B. – Hull – wheat.
January 3	1920	Twelve months time charter.

S.S.W.I. Radcliffe

June 3	1919	Tyne – Porto Ferraio – coal.
August 8	1919	Buenos Aires – Avonmouth – wheat.
October 3	1919	Twelve months time charter to Hudson's Bay Co.
November 16	1920	Newport – Freemantle – in ballast.

S.S. Clarissa Radcliffe

May 8	1919	South Shields – Porto Ferraio – coal.
July 8	1919	Buenos Aires – Hull – linseed.
September 17	1919	Hull – Hampton Roads – in ballast.
October 8	1919	Norfolk, Va. – Gibraltar – coal.
December 8	1919	Gibraltar – Montevideo – in ballast.
January 8	1920	Plate – Avonmouth – wheat and maize.
March 11	1920	Twelve months charter to Italian Government.

S.S. Llangorse

June 6	1919	Tyne – Naples – coal.
July 29	1919	Montreal – Limerick – wheat and flour.
September 3	1919	Twelve months charter.
September 21	1920	Cardiff – Hampton Roads – in ballast.
October 15	1920	Norfolk, Va. – St. Nazaire – coal.
November 25	1920	Barry – Philadelphia – in ballast.
December 29	1920	Philadelphia – Salerno – wheat.

Many of the Cardiff-owned ships were laid up for extended periods. As one Cardiff docksman vividly sums up the period 1920 – 25[15] *One day coal and cargo space were in demand; the next day nobody wanted either. Soon a number of shipping companies were rumoured to be in difficulties quickly followed by the announcement that the largest of the newcomers . . . had sunk, taking with it the wartime savings of thousands of small investors, many of them thrifty and hopeful South Walians. The tiers of laid-up ships, the silent ship repair yards and the groups of unemployed seamen outside the Shipping Office by the Dock gates were a depressing site.* In 1919 and 1920 many of Radcliffe's vessels were time chartered to other companies, but 1921 saw the slump really biting with the result that many of the company's vessels were laid up for extended periods simply because no cargoes were available to them. In 1921, for example, the *Boverton* was laid up at West Hartlepool for most of the year; the *W. I. Radcliffe* was laid up at Cardiff for six months; while the *Llanberis* and *Llangollen* were idle for most of the year in Newport Docks. Despite this, some of the Radcliffe vessels were fully occupied during the first few years of the 1920s, although substantial losses were made on many of the voyages. The new vessel, the *Ethel Radcliffe*, the pride and joy of the fleet, was not laid up at all and undertook voyages to all parts of the world:

December 11	1920	Barry – Port Said – coal.
March 9	1921	Mauritius – London – sugar.
June 4	1921	Norfolk, Virginia – Immingham – coal.
August 16	1921	Texas City – Antwerp – wheat.
October 28	1921	Cardiff – Port Said – coal.
December 9	1921	Cardiff – Port Said – coal.
February 18	1922	Baltimore – Hamburg – wheat.
March 29	1922	Cardiff – Port Said – coal.
July 2	1922	Buenos Aires – Hamburg – wheat.
August 31	1922	Cardiff – Portland, Maine – coal.
October 11	1922	Galveston – Genoa (Civita Vecchia) – wheat.
January 17	1923	Bahia Blanca – Genoa – wheat and oats.
March 22	1923	Cardiff – Hamburg – coal.
May 5	1923	Barry – Port Said – coal.
July 7	1923	Karachi – Bombay – Leith – Antwerp – grain, ore, general.
September 8	1923	Barry – Rio de Janeiro – coal.
October 4	1923	Rio de Janeiro – Baltimore – ore.
December 5	1923	Norfolk, Va. – Genoa – grain.
February 14	1924	Bahia Blanca – London – wheat, oats, linseed
April 18	1924	Barry – Santos – coal.
July 29	1924	Rosario – Buenos Aires – Belfast – maize, bran.
November 7	1924	Galveston – Genoa – wheat.

Despite the fact that some of the vessels were in constant employ in the early twenties, the golden era was obviously over and the annual reports of the various single ship companies that made up Evan Thomas, Radcliffe & Company reflect the general gloom and depression that seemed to have prevailed among Cardiff shipowners in the early twenties. For example, in 1921 the annual report of the Ethel Radcliffe Steamship Company speaks of *a critical period of inactivity and depression. The coal strike, with its disastrous consequences and rates and freight in practically all the markets of the world have dropped to a level that make it impossible to leave a margin of profit and trading; in fact in many cases there are serious losses rendering it necessary to lay up a large section of British shipping.* In 1922 things were even worse for *the shipping industry has passed through a period of unparalleled depression . . . there is no prospect of immediate improvement.* The message of doom was repeated throughout the twenties although in 1925 there was a slight air of optimism in the air, for although *the current year has been one of unprecedented difficulty and depression . . . the general condition of the freight market has been worse than it has been in the whole of our experience . . . we can only hope that better times are in store.*

Peterston 1925

In anticipation of those better times, Evan Thomas Radcliffe surprisingly began to invest money in new vessels in 1925. The *Gileston* (built 1898), the *Llangollen* (built 1900), the *Llangorse* (built 1904) and the *Picton* (built 1906) were sold soon after the delivery of the new vessels. The four new vessels to be launched in 1925 were:

(i) *Peterston* (gross tons 4680) built by Bartram & Sons, South Dock, Sunderland. Cost £84,647.

Flimston 1925

(ii) *Flimston* (gross tons 4674) built by Bartram & Sons, South Dock, Sunderland. Cost £84,250.
(iii) *Vera Radcliffe* (gross tons 5587) built by Craig Taylor & Co., Stockton-on-Tees. Cost £99,439.
(iv) *Catherine Radcliffe* (gross tons 5589) built by Craig Taylor & Co., Stockton-on-Tees. Cost £99,439.

The new vessels were considerably cheaper than the *Ethel Radcliffe* of 1920, built when the prices of new and old ships were greatly inflated. Nevertheless, in the 1920s substantial losses were made in the trading of all the vessels.

The *Catherine Radcliffe*, named after Daniel Radcliffe's daughter, was delivered in February 1925 and left Newport for Bahia Blanca with a cargo of coal under the command of Capt. John Davies of Llangrannog, Ceredigion. She then sailed in ballast to Durban transporting a cargo of coal to Port Sudan. This first voyage resulted in a loss of £1,352. The second voyage began with the vessel sailing from Port Sudan to Karachi and Bombay returning to Swansea and Hull with a cargo of ore. She then sailed from Barry to Santos with coal, then to Calera Caloso, and Antofagasta with nitrates for Mobile. She then transported coal from Newport, Va., to Rio de Janeiro and ended the second voyage at Rotterdam, having carried a cargo of wheat from Bahia Blanca. This voyage resulted in a loss of £2,144.

The *Vera Radcliffe*, also named after Daniel Radcliffe's daughter was commanded by Capt. M. Mathias of Cardigan and left Barry on her maiden voyage with coal for Buenos Aires. She then visited a number of ports on the west coast of South America – Iquique, Pisagua and Caldera to transport nitrates to

Vera and Catherine Radcliffe: Daniel Radcliffe's two daughters

Wilmington, Delaware. The vessel then took a cargo of coal from Newport, Va., to Rio de Janeiro. This first voyage resulted in a loss of £2,960.

The *Peterston*, captained by J. E. Owen of Swansea, left on a long maiden voyage on 25 February, 1925 taking coal from Barry to Bahia Blanca, sailing in ballast to Durban to load coal for Colombo. The vessel then visited a number of ports in the East Indies taking sugar to Bombay and returning to London with wheat from Karachi. The loss on this voyage of nearly a year's duration amounted to £1,612.

The *Flimston*, delivered in May 1925 and commanded by Capt. S. H. Mathias of Newport, Pembrokeshire, took coal from Barry to Bahia Blanca, returning to Europe with a cargo of wheat and oats to Genoa. Although the vessel was fully occupied through the whole of this maiden voyage for she did not have to sail in ballast at all, the loss was still £1,775.

Henry and Daniel Radcliffe

In the early 1920s Henry Radcliffe, one of the founders of the Company, died at the age of 66 years at his home in Druidstone, St. Mellons. He left a son, Wyndham Ivor Radcliffe, and two daughters, Clarissa Gwendoline Gwynne Maitland and Sarah Ethel Radcliffe. He was an extensive owner of land in the Vale of Glamorgan. *Of late years,* says his obituary in the *Western Mail* of 17 December, 1921 *Mr. Radcliffe expended many thousands of pounds on the purchase of farms . . . In June 1916 he purchased the Aubrey Estates in the Vale extending nearly 7,000 acres and located in 22 parishes.* In his will he left a total of over £1¼m and he was a shareholder in a large number of companies in South Wales including the following: Taff Vale Railway; Barry Railway Co.; Vale of Glamorgan Railway Co.; Tempus Shipping Co.; Cardiff Port Iron & Coal Storage Co.; North's Navigation Collieries Ltd.; Great Western Colliery Co. Ltd.; P. & A. Campbell Ltd.; Cambrian Railways; Alexandra Docks Newport and Guest Keen & Nettlefolds, in addition to being a Director of the 30 single-ship companies that made up Evan Thomas Radcliffe. In 1921, however, with the difficulties experienced in shipping, 18 of those companies were liquidated and Henry Radcliffe *received about £600,000 as shareholder and £367,000 based on twenty years of management fees as compensation for loss of management.*[16]

With Henry Radcliffe's death the chairmanship of the company passed on to his younger brother Daniel of Tal-y-werydd, Penylan, Cardiff. He was to control the company until his death on 29 March, 1933. Daniel Radcliffe was a very influential figure in Cardiff Docks and was a director of 26 companies, all of them associated with shipping. The two vessels *Catherine Radcliffe* and *Vera Radcliffe* of 1925 were named after his two daughters. *He was*, said an editorial in the Western Mail on 30 March, 1933 *one of the most lovable of men. Entering a shipowner's office when a lad, when the port was growing rapidly to fame, the great transition from sail to steam and the development of the steam ship had still to be accomplished, his business career may be said to have been contemporaneous with the rise of Cardiff as one of the largest tonnage-owning ports in the world. He flourished in the spacious days of British shipping, before the aftermath of the war brought depression and loss, a keen business instinct was needed in the best of times to build up a great and successful fleet and it is to men of the late Mr. Radcliffe's enterprise and spirit the British shipping industry owes the position it has won as the most efficient, reliable and wide-spread carrying agency that the world has ever known. A keener instinct still was needed to meet the crisis of world depression and it is to men of Mr. Radcliffe's faith, good council and cheerful moods that the British shipping industry was looking for guidance and support. His death will be a great loss to the industry.*
This is a man not only a shipping magnate the world who knew him will mourn.

Controlling a large fleet of cargo steamers his name was known in the far places of the Earth and wherever the ships of his firm sailed there also travelled the famed Dan Radcliffe as a man of boundless generosity and genial personality. He gave a fortune to charity. His gifts for the advancement of education were on a princely scale. His private benefactions of which one hears must have been a tax even upon his purse. No good cause, whether religious, cultural or sporting looked to him for support in vain. The secret of his popularity was not in his generosity but in his own personality. He possessed the divine gift of friendship in a remarkable degree and it was this that won for him the affection and esteem of his fellows.

New Investments

The twenties and early thirties was a period of unrelieved gloom for Cardiff shipowners and it says a great deal for the business acumen of the directors of Evan Thomas Radcliffe that they were able to ride out the storm when so many other shipping companies were going under. Although in 1926 *a better demand for tonnage became manifest* by 1927 the company's report regretted that *the improvement in freight generally . . . has not been sustained and latterly the freight market has collapsed . . . and it is difficult to find remunerative employment for tonnage.* By 1930 the depression had really set in with *the shipping industry passing through a period of unprecedented and acute depression, trading conditions being so bad that it has been impossible to avoid working without loss with the result that in common with other owners, it has been found necessary to lay our vessels up for long periods during the year . . . there is no alternative to further laying up of steamers.*

Nevertheless, even in those unpromising times, Evan Thomas Radcliffe invested heavily in new ships and in 1928 – 29 they built as many as eight ships. They were:

(a) *Llanberis* (Gross registered tons – 5055). Built by Hawthorn, Leslie & Co., Wallsend-on-Tyne. No. 549. Cost of building – £86,753. Launched 12 October, 1927 by Mrs. Shirley St. Clare. Master – R. Roberts, Aberdyfi, Gwynedd.

(b) *Llandilo* (Gross registered tons – 4966). Built by Bartram & Sons, Sunderland. No. 262. Cost of building – £86,913. Launched 6 February, 1926, by Mrs. B. T. Morris. Master T. Jones, Aberarth, Dyfed.

(c) *Llanfair* (Gross registered tons – 4966). Built by Bartram & Sons, Sunderland. No. 263. Cost of building – £85,077. Launched 4 May, 1928 by Mrs. Pinkney. Master – S. H. Mathias, Newport, Dyfed.

(d) *Llangollen* (Gross registered tons – 5055). Built Hawthorn, Leslie & Co., Wallsend-on-Tyne. No. 550. Cost of building – £86,990. Launched 24 November, 1927 by Mrs. H. E. Paradise. Master – D. G. Evans, New Quay, Dyfed.

(e) *Llanover* (Gross registered tons – 4979). Built Bartram & Son, Sunderland. No. 261. Cost of building £86,765. Launched 24 November, 1927 by Mrs. Shirley St. Clare. Master – John James, Aberporth, Dyfed.

Llanfair 1928

Llangollen 1928

(f) *Llanwern* (Gross registered tons – 4966). Built Bartram & Son, Sunderland. No. 264. Cost of building – £85,422. Launched 1 September, 1928 by Mrs. Bartram. Master – D. G. Clark, Plymouth, Devon.

(g) *Llanarth* (Gross registered tons 5053). Built Bartram & Son, Sunderland. No. 265. Cost of building £82,579. Launched 24 January, 1920 by Mrs. Rosa Bartram. Master – J. R. Jenkins, Aber-porth, Dyfed.

(h) *Llanishen* (Gross registered tons – 5052). Built Bartram & Son, Sunderland. No. 266. Cost of building – £82,568. Launched 25 April, 1929 by Mrs. Harbottle. Master – Richard Roberts, Aberdyfi, Gwynedd.

The eight new vessels were engaged in a world-wide tramping trade; the following being a summary of the first five voyages of each ship.

In 1931, the Radcliffe fleet consisted of 16 vessels:

Llanberis (1928)
Llanover (1928)
Clarissa Radcliffe (1915)
Ethel Radcliffe (1920)
Peterston (1925)
Llanarth (1929)
Llanfair (1929)
Wimborne (1911)
Llangollen (1929)
Catherine Radcliffe (1925
Llanwern (1928)
Llandilo (1928)
Flimston (1925)
Llanishen (1929)
Vera Radcliffe (1925)
W. I. Radcliffe (1913)

All was not well, however, for most of the vessels were laid up for considerable periods in the early thirties. In 1930 and 1931, for example, the *W. I. Radcliffe* was laid up for a total of 270 days at Newport, the *Clarissa Radcliffe* for 370 days at Barry and the *Vera Radcliffe* for 375 days at Cardiff. Even the newer vessels were idle for the *Llanfair, Llandilo, Llanwern, Llanarth* and *Llanishen* spent extended periods of idleness at Barry Docks.

Llanashe 1936

Llandaff 1937

With Henry C. Bolter and J. Allen Pratt as directors, the firm of E. T. Radcliffe rode out the storm and 1930 saw a small profit accruing to the company and with the addition of a government subsidy for shipping in 1935, things improved considerably and all the firm's vessels were fully occupied once again; indeed, confidence was such that in 1936 – 7 two new vessels were purchased from Bartrams of Sunderland. They were:

Llanashe (Gross tonnage 4835). Delivered 18 November 1936. Master – W. R. Burgess, Cardiff. Cost £79,979.
Llandaff (Gross tonnage 4826). Delivered 19 May 1937. Master – J. R. Jenkins, Aber-porth, Cardigan. Cost – £80,542.

In the meantime the *Catherine Radcliffe* was wrecked off the Japanese coast and the *Wimborne* and *W. I. Radcliffe* were both sold to other companies. The two new vessels were successful as appreciable profits were made on each voyage, for example, from its delivery in 1937 until September 1939, the *Llandaff* made the following:

Voyage 1. Tyne – Port Said – Poti – Baltimore. Profit £10,880.
Voyage 1A. Time Charter. Profit £19,351.
Voyage 2. Huelva, Baltimore – Montreal – Cape Town, Assumption Island – Auckland. Profit £6,379.
Voyage 3. Barry – Alexandria – Freemantle – Brisbane – London. Profit £15,157.

An indication of the trading pattern of Radcliffe ships in the inter-war period may be obtained from the diaries of Capt. Daniel Jenkins of Swansea, a native of Tresaith, near Cardigan, Dyfed who began his seafaring career in 1920.

17.10.1920 Cosmos (The Cosmos Trading Co., London) Ordinary Seaman. Master – Daniel Jenkins, Tresaith, Dyfed. Paid off Garston, 15.5.1920.

20.11.1920 Trevelyan (Edward Hain & Co., St. Ives) Ordinary Seaman. Master – Ben Evans, Cardigan. Paid off Cardiff, 31.12.1920

18.12.1921 Trevince (Edward Hain, St. Ives, Cornwall) Able Seaman. Master – Ben Evans, Cardigan. Paid off Falmouth 24.10.1921.

31.1.1922 Wimborne (Evan Thomas Radcliffe) – Able Seaman. to 9.8.1922 Master – J. W. Jones, Blaenannerch, near Cardigan.
Signed on Newport 31.1.1922
Newport – loaded coal to Port Said – water ballast to Barry.
Barry – loaded coal for Port Said – water ballast to Newport.
Newport – loaded coal for Port Said – water ballast to Gibraltar for orders and bunkers.
Gibraltar – ballast to Hampton Roads, U.S.A. Bunkered at Norfolk, VA. to Philadelphia.
Philadelphia – loaded full cargo of wheat for Antwerp.
Antwerp – discharged. Water ballast to Barry.
Paid off 9.8.1922.

11.1.1923 Highland Loch (Messrs. H. & W. Nelson, Ltd., London) Quartermaster. Master – H. Lloyd, Caernarfon. Paid off London 14.2.1923.

7.9.1923 Ethel Radcliffe (Evan Thomas Radcliffe) Able seaman. Master – M. Mathias, Cardigan.
Signed on Barry 7.9.1923.
Barry – loaded coal for Rio De Janeiro.
Rio De Janeiro – discharged and loaded full cargo of manganese ore for Baltimore, U.S.A.
After leaving Rio, discovered five stowaways. Transferred them at sea to S.S. Llangorse outward bound for Rio.
Baltimore – discharged and water ballast to Newport News, Va.
Newport News. Vessel dry-docked and water ballast to Norfolk, Va.
Norfolk – loaded full cargo of wheat for Genoa.
Genoa – discharged and water ballast to Bahia Blanca via Algiers for bunkers.
Bahia Blanca – loaded full cargo of wheat, oats and barley for

London via Las Palmas for bunkers.
London (Victoria Dock) – discharged to lighters, water ballast to Barry.
Paid off 1.4.1924.

27.8.1924 – Highland Loch (Messrs. H. W. Nelson Ltd., London). Quartermaster.
Paid off London – 26.10.1924.

26.2.1925 – Peterston (Evan Thomas Radcliffe). Able Seaman.
Master – J. E. Owen, Swansea.
Signed on Sunderland 26.2.1925 – Maiden voyage.
Sunderland to Barry in ballast.
Barry – loaded coal for Bahia Blanca.
Bahia Blanca – discharged and water ballast to Durban.
Durban – loaded coal for Colombo.
Colombo – discharged and water ballast to Java.
Probolingo, Surabaya & Samarane – loaded full cargo of sugar in bags for Bombay via Colombo for bunkers.
Bombay – discharged Victoria Dock and water ballast to Karachi.
Karachi – loaded full cargo of wheat in bags for London via Aden, Port Said, Malta and Algiers for bunkers.
London – discharged at Rank's Mills, Victoria Dock.
Water ballast to Sunderland.
Paid off Sunderland – 12.10.1925.

26.11.1925 – King Edward (King Line Ltd.). Able Seaman.
Master – M. Ritch, Stromness, Orkney.
Paid off Hull 25.2.1926.

22.8.1926 – Withington (The Times S.S. Co., Cardiff). Second Mate.
Master – S. Jones, Nefyn, Gwynedd.
Paid off Cardiff – 27.9.1926.

30.6.1927 – Wimborne (Evan Thomas Radcliffe). Third Mate.
Master – J. R. Jenkins, Aberporth, Cardigan.
Cardiff – loaded coal for Alexandria.
Alexandria – discharged and sailed in ballast for Algiers for orders and bunkers.
Algiers – Portland (Oregon) via Panama Canal.
Portland – full cargo of wheat for Hull and Leith via St. Thomas (West Indies) for bunkers.
Leith – in ballast to Dunstan-on-Tyne.
Loaded coal for Oran.
Oran – discharged and sailed in ballast for Bahia Blanca.
Bahia Blanca – loaded wheat and barley for London and Emden via

St. Vincent (Cape Verde Islands) for bunkers.
Emden – in ballast for Cardiff.
Paid off Cardiff 7 April 1928.

25.6.1928 – Llanfair (Evan Thomas Radcliffe) – Second Mate Master – S. H. Mathias, Newport, Pembrokeshire.
Sunderland – in ballast for Dunstan-on-Tyne.
Dunstan – loaded coal for Port Said.
Port Said – sailed in ballast to Algiers for orders.
Algiers – Havana in ballast.
Cayo Mambi & Port Padre (Cuba) – loaded brown sugar in bags for Lands End for orders.
Liverpool (Sandon Dock) – discharged and sailed in ballast to Newport, Mon.
Newport – loaded coal for Alexandria.
Alexandria – in ballast to Java.
Problingo – Surabaya – Pitsruan – Semarane – loaded sugar in bags for Alexandria via Colombo & Perim for bunkers.
Alexandria – discharged sugar. Sailed in ballast for Marmagoa (India).
Marmagoa – loaded manganese ore and groundnuts for Hamburg and Antwerp via Perim, Port Said & Algiers for bunkers.
Antwerp to Cardiff in ballast.
Cardiff (Queen Alexandra Dock) – loaded coal for Port Said.
Port Said – in ballast to Newport, Mon.
Newport – loaded coal for Alexandria.
Alexandria – in ballast to Newport.
Newport – loaded coal for Alexandria.
Alexandria – in ballast to Barry.
Left vessel 26.8.1929 to sit for Master's Certificate.

30.5.1930 – St. Quentin (St. Quentin Shipping Co., Cardiff). First Mate. Master – J. D. Jones, Penfedw, Brongest, Newcastle Emlyn, Dyfed.

9.5.1932 – Llanover (Evan Thomas Radcliffe). Second Mate Master – J. E. Thomas, Cwmcou, Newcastle Emlyn, Dyfed. Joined and paid off at Sunderland – transferred to Ethel Radcliffe as first mate at Barry.

12.5.1932 – Ethel Radcliffe (Evan Thomas Radcliffe). First mate. Master – John O. Davies, Ffynnonwen, Penmorfa, Cardigan.
Barry – loaded coal for Buenos Aires.
Buenos Aires – maize and linseed for St. Vincent for orders.
Amsterdam – discharged. Left for Barry in ballast.
Paid off Barry – 15.8.1932.

10.10.1932 – Peterston (Evan Thomas Radcliffe). Second Mate. Master – J. Parry, Pensarn, Aberdaron, Gwynedd.
Cardiff (Queen's Dock) – loaded coal for Marseilles.
Marseilles – discharged. Sailed in ballast to Constanza via Istanbul.
Constanza – loaded full cargo of grain for Rotterdam. Sailed in ballast to Dunston-on-Tyne (3.12.1932).
Dunston – loaded coal for Savona.
Savona – sailed in ballast to Constanza via Istanbul.
Constanza – loaded grain for Hamburg via Algiers for bunkers.
Hamburg – discharged and sailed in ballast to Barry Roads.
Cardiff (Queens Dock) – loaded coal for Havana and sailed in ballast to Nuevitas.
Nuevitas – loaded sugar for London.
London – discharged at Woolwich Buoys and sailed in ballast to Barry.
Barry – laid up for five months.
26.9.1933 – Barry – loaded coal for Genoa.
Genoa – discharged and sailed for Istanbul in ballast.
Istanbul – orders to proceed to Nicolaieff.
Nicolaieff – loaded full cargo of wheat for Falmouth for orders via Ceuta for bunkers.
Hull – discharged grain. Sailed in ballast to Sunderland.
Sunderland – six weeks converting engines to superheat by Messrs. J. Dickinson.
Sunderland – sailed 27.1.1934 with coal for Algiers.
Algiers – sailed in ballast for Colombo for orders.
Vizagapatam – loaded 700 ton oil-cake and groundnuts and sailed to Cocanada.
Cocanada – loaded full cargo of groundnuts and oil cake for Port Said for orders.
Port Said – orders to proceed to Liverpool via Algiers for bunkers.
Liverpool – discharged part cargo and sailing for Rotterdam.
Rotterdam – discharged and dry docked at Schiedam. Pontoon and sailed in ballast for Immingham.
Immingham. Paid off 12.5.1934.
19.11.1936 – Wimborne (Evan Thomas Radcliffe). First Mate. Master H. A. Denham, Tilehurst, Reading and T. Jones, Plas, Aberarth, Cardigan.
Barry – in ballast for Buenos Aires Roads for orders.
San Lorenzo – loaded 200 tons cereals.
Rosario – loaded 4,000 tons cereals.
Buenos Aires – completed loading, sailed for Avonmouth via Las

Palmas for bunkering.
Avonmouth – discharged. Sailed for Barry in ballast.
Barry (T. Jones as new master) – loaded coal for Rio De Janeiro.
Rio De Janeiro – discharged and sailed for La Plata in ballast.
La Plata – loaded wheat in bulk for Shanghai via Durban, Batavia & Keelong.
Durban – discharged No. 5 hold to find leak in ship's side. 11 days at Durban.
Batavia & Keelong – Bunkered.
Shanghai – discharged and sailed in ballast to Calcutta.
Calcutta – loaded coal for Bombay.
Bombay – Discharged and sailed to Calcutta in ballast.
Calcutta – loaded coal for Marmagoa.
Marmagoa – discharged and sailed to Aden in ballast.
Aden – loaded full cargo of salt in bulk for Calcutta.
Calcutta – discharged and loaded coal for Madras and Negapatam.
Negapatam – discharged and sailed in ballast for Saigon.
Saigon – loaded full cargo of maize and rice in bags for Dunkirk, Havre & Rouen via Sabang, Perim and Port Said for bunkering.
Oran – bad coal and adverse weather conditions – obliged to call at Oran.
Dunkirk, Havre & Rouen – discharged and sailed to Barry in ballast.
Barry – paid off 16.12.1935.

12.3.1936 – Llanashe (Evan Thomas Radcliffe). First Mate Masters – W. R. Burgess, Mayfield Avenue, Cardiff, D. G. Evans, Greenhills, New Quay, Dyfed.
Maiden voyage Sunderland in ballast to Dunstan-on-Tyne.
Dunstan – trials run loaded off Tyne. Gibraltar with coal.
Gibraltar – sailed in ballast to Buenos Aires.
San Lorenzo & Rosario – loaded grain for Madeira for orders.
Avonmouth – discharged to Spillers' New Mill.
Cardiff – sailed in ballast for British Columbia via Panama.
Loaded timber at New Westminster, Vancouver, Nanaima, & Crofton, Vancouver Island for Sydney, N.S.W.
Sydney – sailed in ballast for Port Kembla.
Port Kembla – bunkered and railed for Geelong.
Geelong – loaded full cargo of wheat in bulk and bags in shelter deck.
Durban – for bunkers, sailed Las Palmas for bunkers and orders.
Falmouth – anchored 26 hours before proceeding to London (Rank's Mills, Victoria Dock) and Hull.

Hull – drydocked, bunkered and sailed for Archangel in ballast.
Archangel – loaded cargo of timber for Port Elizabeth & Lourenço Marques via Tyne for bunkers.
Tyne – Bunkered at Commissions taiths on Friday, 5 November. Sailed 11pm Saturday 6 November. 1 fireman paid off, 2 cleared off. Had to anchor outside Tyne Piers from midday Saturday to 10pm Sunday, 7 November for crew to sober up for duty.
Port Elizabeth – discharged part cargo, completed discharging Lourenço Marques
Lourenço Marques – loaded coal for Capetown.
Capetown – discharged coal and sailed for Durban in ballast.
Durban – loaded coal for Capetown.
Three voyages with coal from Durban to Capetown.
Lourenço Marques – loaded coal for Hong Kong via Sabang.
Sabang – bunkered.
Hong Kong – discharged coal and sailed to Suva in ballast.
Suva & Lavtuka – loaded sugar for Lands End for orders via Panama Canal & Jamaica.
About halfway across Pacific Ocean Capt. Evans slipped and broke his right leg. Re-set as best we could, made canvas cradle to rest leg on. He remained in that position all the way to London. It took us 6 weeks to reach London.
Bunkered at Cristobal.
Port Royal, Jamaica – bunkered and sailed via Crooked Passage & Great Circle to Lands End.
London – discharged at Charlton Buoys.
London – left for Blyth (with Capt. H. Roberts as Master) to load.
5.9.1938 – Blyth – paid off and came home to study for Sanitary Inspector's Exam.

In 1939 the Radcliffe fleet consisted of 15 vessels:

Llanberis (Built 1928)	5055 GRT
Llangollen (Built 1928)	5056 GRT
Llanover (Built 1928)	4949 GRT
Ethel Radcliffe (Built 1920)	5673 GRT
Vera Radcliffe (Built 1925)	5587 GRT
Clarissa Radcliffe (Built 1915)	5754 GRT
Llanashe (Built 1936)	4836 GRT
Llanwern (Built 1928)	4966 GRT
Llandilo (Built 1928)	4966 GRT
Peterston (Built 1925)	4680 GRT

Flimston (Built 1925)	4674 GRT
Llanarth (Built 1929)	5053 GRT
Llanishen (Built 1929)	5053 GRT
Llandaff (Built 1937)	4825 GRT
Llanfair (Built 1928)	4966 GRT

Ships' Crews

Like many another Cardiff shipping company Radcliffe's drew heavily on the coastal villages of Cardigan Bay for men to man the vessels. As the coastal trade in West and North Wales declined in the late nineteenth century many of the mariners of those regions began sailing in Cardiff vessels, although most of them still retained their homes in their villages of origin. Capt. B. T. Morris, who for many years was a Marine Superintendent with Radcliffes, was typical of the masters that served with the company. He was a native of the small West Wales hamlet of Bryngwyn, the second son of a master mariner who sailed regularly from the nearby village of Aberporth. In 1886 Ben Morris, at the age of 16 years, went to sea as a 'Boy' on board the barque *Onward*, commanded by another Cardigan man, David Morris. *We sailed to Santos in Brazil and we were sailing for over two months before we reached Santos; an unhealthy place with mosquitos eating you up. We remained there for a month before sailing to the Gulf of Mexico. This too was a voyage of about two months and we left Mobile for home with a cargo of grain. I again sailed in the same vessel for Rosario, a voyage that took 90 days. In those days sailing vessels went up the River Plate for about three hundred miles and this took almost a month. We sailed to the Gulf of Mexico and arrived in Cardiff after a voyage of 15 months. Nothing untoward happened on my first voyage except that the Chief Officer from Aberporth died and we buried him at sea. . . In 1892 I joined the vessel commanded by Capt. D. Jones of Aberporth. Among the crew were two Aberporth boys and myself as A.B.s and a mate from Tresaith.*[17] Whereas Ben Morris's father was concerned exclusively with the coastal trade sailing principally from Aber-porth to the ports of South Wales and the Bristol Channel, by the time his son began his seafaring career, the West Wales coastal trade was on the wane and more and more of the sailors of West Wales were sailing deep sea, principally with Cardiff shipping firms. B. T. Morris, who obtained his master's ticket, sailed aboard the following vessels:

Vessel	*Llanberis*	*Llandilo*
Voyage No. 1	Delivered 12.1.1928 Tyne Dock – Algiers (coal) Rosario & Buenos Aires – London (grain)	Delivered 28.5.1928 Tyne Dock – Algiers (coal) Rosario, San Nicolas, La Plata – Hamburg (grain)
Voyage No. 2	Newport – Alexandria (coal) Marmagoa – Hamburg & (general)	West Hartlepool – Leghorn (coal) Cuba – London (sugar)

Voyage No. 3	Tyne – Bona (coal)	Cardiff – Port Said (coal) Geelong, Milazzo (Sicily) – Birkenhead (wheat)
Voyage No. 4	Barry – La Plata (coal) Rosario, Buenos Aires – Dunkirk, Hamburg (grain)	Newport – Alexandria (coal)
Voyage No. 5	Tyne – Port Said (coal) Madras Coast – Rotterdam & Bremen (groundnuts)	Newport – Alexandria (coal)

Vessel	*Llanfair*	*Llangollen*
Voyage No. 1	Delivered 3.7.1928 Dunston-on-Tyne – Port Said (coal) Cuba – Liverpool (sugar)	Delivered 25.2.1928 Tyne – Port Said (coal) Karachi – Rotterdam & Bremen (grain, seeds, etc.)
Voyage No. 2	Newport – Alexandria (coal) Java – Alexandria (sugar) Marmagoa – Hamburg & Antwerp (ground nuts, ore)	Newport – Alexandria (coal) Rosario, Buenos Aires – Hull (grain)
Voyage No. 3	Cardiff – Port Said (coal)	Tyne – Algiers (coal) Galveston – Havre & Brake (wheat & barley)
Voyage No. 4	Newport – Alexandria (coal)	Cardiff – Port Said (coal) Madras Coast – Bremen (groundnuts)
Voyage No. 5	Newport – Alexandria (coal)	Newport – Alexandria (coal)

Vessel	*Llanover*	*Llanwern*
Voyage No. 1	Delivered 3.3.1928 Sunderland – Savona (coal) Rosario & La Plata – Rotterdam (grain)	Delivered 5.10.1928 Tyne – Santos (coal & firebricks) Rosario, Buenos Avonmouth (grain)
Voyage No. 2	Newport – Alexandria (coal) Rosario, Buenos Aires – London (grain)	Cardiff – Rio de Janeiro (coal) Bahia Blanca – Hamburg (wheat, barley, linseed)
Voyage No. 3	Cardiff – Buenos Aires (coal) Buenos Aires – Avonmouth (maize) London (grain)	Barry – Rio de Janeiro (coal) Villa Constitution, Buenos Aires (grain)
Voyage No. 4	Barry – Rio de Janeiro (coal) Bahia Blanca – Hamburg (wheat)	Barry – Rio de Janeiro (coal)

Voyage No. 5	Dunston-on-Tyne – Port Said (coal) Rosario, Buenos Aires – London (maize)	Barry – Buenos Aires (coal) San Pedro, Villa Constitution, Buenos Aires – Avonmouth (grain)

Vessel	*Llanarth*	*Llanishen*
Voyage No. 1	Delivered 30.3.1929 Tyne – Oran (coal) San Lorenzo – Buenos Aires – Aires – Rotterdam (grain)	Delivered 19.6.1929 Tyne – Santos (coal) San Lorenzo, La Plata – London (grain)
Voyage No. 2	Newport – Alexandria (coal)	Barry – Rio de Janeiro (coal)
Voyage No. 3	Barry – Montevideo (coal) Rosario, Buenos Aires – London	Cardiff – Montevideo (coal)
Voyage No. 4	Barry – Leghorn (coal)	Barry – Port Said (coal) Kherson & Nicolaieff – Emdon & Bremen (barley)
Voyage No. 5	Cardiff – Buenos Aires (coal) Bahia Blanca – Antwerp (grain)	Rosario, Buenos Aires – Avonmouth (maize)

1886 – 1890. *Onward* (558 GRT). Master – D. Morris (of Cardigan) as Boy, Ordinary Seaman and A.B.
1890 – 2. *River Nith* (1165 GRT). Master – D. Jones (of Aberporth) as A.B.
1893 – 4. *Regnant* (1244 GRT). Masters – J. Jenkins (of Llangrannog), D. Morgan (of Tresaith) as 2nd Mate and 1st Mate.
1894 – 5. *Holderness* (1099 GRT). Master – W. Massam.
1896 – . *Douglas Hill* (2171 GRT). Masters – W. Williams and W. Evans (of New Quay) as 2nd Mate.
1896 – 7. *Ethel Radcliffe* (2874 GRT) Master – T. J. Owen (of Llangrannog) as Mate.
1897 – 8. *Douglas Hill* (2171 GRT) Master W. Evans (of New Quay) as 2nd Mate.
1898 – 9. *Ethel Radcliffe* (2874 GRT) Master T. J. Owen (of Llangrannog) as Mate.
1899 – 1900. *Windsor* (4074 GRT) Master – B. Parry; as Mate.

For the next twelve years Capt. Morris served as Master of a number of Radcliffe ships including the *Iolo*, the *Jane Radcliffe, Llanberis* (of 1910), *Picton* and *Wimborne*, before becoming Marine Superintendent for the company in 1912. He was to remain in that post until he was 70 years of age.

It was not unusual to find a large proportion of the crew of a particular vessel coming from the same village in North or West Wales. Many a sailor sailed *with Capt. Owen, Aber-porth or Capt. Evans, New Quay* rather than on a particular ship. Father and son, brothers and cousins, brothers-in-law and uncles often sailed together on the same vessel. With a Welsh-speaking master and a Welsh-speaking crew the language of messroom and saloon was often Welsh, but the language of instruction and business aboard ship was invariably English. Quite often hymn-singing sessions, Sunday Schools and even prayer meetings were held on board ship and life aboard a Cardiff tramp steamer could almost be regarded as an extension of the social and cultural activities of 'home'. Chapel-going, temperate master mariners like Capt. Morris were regarded as 'good influences' by members of village communities in West Wales and many a young seaman took his first voyage in ships under the command of such worthy men that were known to the community.

Lists of crews (random samples)

Llandaff – 1938–9. Voyage 2.
Master – J. R. Jenkins, Aber-porth
Mate – D. Williams, Llangrannog
Alun Jones, Holyhead (at Montreal)
2nd Mate – Evan Owens, Llangrannog
3rd Mate – J. J. Carrol, Halifax
Engineer – J. Mummery, Cardiff
2nd Engineer – J. Dove, Barry
3rd Engineer – S. Cooper, Port Talbot (deserted 2.2.39)
4th Engineer – A. Townsend, Hull
Steward – A. Ball, Hull
Cook – J. H. Lewis, Hull (deserted 2.2.39 at Auckland)

Llandaff – 1940–1. Voyage 5
Master – J. R. Jenkins, Aber-porth
Mate – A. Jones, Holyhead
2nd Mate – A. G. Pope, Alberta, Canada
3rd Mate – M. J. Peyton, Watford
Engineer – J. Mummery, Cardiff
2nd Engineer – D. M. Sanderson, Norton-on-Tees
3rd Engineer – J. G. Jones, Cardigan
4th Engineer – W. G. Jackson, Salford
Steward – C. Thompson, Cardiff
Cook – J. Richards, Aber-porth

Llangollen – February to May 1914. Voyage 56
Master – R. Roberts, Holyhead
Mate – W. Morgan, Cardiff
2nd Mate – J. E. Davies, Llangrannog, Cardigan
Engineer – R. E. Rosser, Morriston
2nd Engineer – A. H. Larkman, Southampton
3rd Engineer – T. E. Thomas, St. Dogmaels
4th Engineer – E. J. Cleverley, Stockton
Steward – E. Cooper
Cook – M. Augustyn

Llangollen – September–December 1925. Voyage 78
Master – John Williams, Cardiff
1st Mate – James Shippen, Cardiff
2nd Mate – D. J. Jenkins, Aberarth
Engineer – D. L. Davies, Cardigan
2nd Engineer – D. M. Davies, Swansea

3rd Engineer – W. J. John, Swansea
4th Enginer – D. E. Thomas, Swansea
Steward – Evan Lewis, Cardigan
Cook – E. Cockhill

Llangollen – June – October 1930. Voyage 9
Master – D. Williams, Machynlleth
Mate – E. O. Jenkins, Aber-porth
2nd Mate – J. Thomas, Newcastle Emlyn
3rd Mate – K. D. Williams, Cardiff
Engineer – D. P. Edmunds, Plymouth
2nd Engineer – G. E. Bowden, Cardiff
3rd Engineer – R. F. Waters, Newport, Mon.
4th Engineer – M. Williams, Melingriffith
Steward – J. Chopoulos
Cook – S. A. Graves

Llanover – February – September 1935. Voyage 22
Master – J. E. Thomas, Newcastle Emlyn
Mate – D. J. Jenkins, Llangrannog
2nd Mate – W. J. Jones, Pontypool
3rd Mate – I. Foulkes, Pwllheli
Engineer – W. Sutcliffe, South Shields
2nd Engineer – B. Rees, Trehafod
3rd Engineer – D. Fyfe, Barry
4th Engineer – E. J. Jones, Boncath, Pemb.
Steward – J. W. Thomas
Cook – I. Davies

Llanover – 1940 – 41. Voyage 33a
Master – W. R. Burgess, Cardiff
Chief Officer – E. Welburn, Shirehampton
2nd Officer – W. T. Metcalf, Grimsby
3rd Officer – L. H. Green, Jersey
Engineer – W. P. Edwards, Merton
2nd Engineer – R. S. Grieve, Paisley
3rd Engineer – P. Dall, Fife
4th Engineer – J. Healy, Shirehampton
Steward – J. D. Fothergill
Cook – E. T. Holland

Llanberis 1917 – 18. Part Voyage 21
Master – J. E. Owen, Swansea
Mate – J. Lewis, Bristol
2nd Mate – G. Simpson, Stretton, Staffs.

3rd Mate – J. Jones, Aberaeron
Engineer – D. J. Rees, Cardiff
2nd Engineer – G. G. Davies, Cardigan
3rd Engineer – C. C. Galletly, Newport, Mon.
4th Engineer – H. Davies, Tonypandy
Steward – W. R. Raisbrick

Llanberis – 1924–5. Voyage 39
Master – D. J. Davies, Aberarth
Mate – W. C. James, Cardiff
2nd Mate – H. A. Denham, Reading
Engineer – A. E. Lofthouse, Stockton-on-Tees
2nd Engineer – G. G. Davies, Cardigan
3rd Engineer – G. Robinson, South Shields
4th Engineer – T. J. Lewis, Bristol
Steward – M. Alexandros
Cook – A. Pierrie

Peterston – January–October 1925. Voyage 1
Master – J. E. Owen, Swansea
Mate – J. D. Jones, Newcastle Emlyn
2nd Mate – W. J. Wright
Engineer – A. H. Corns, Cardiff
2nd Engineer – G. A. Lewis, Merthyr
3rd Engineer – E. J. Lloyd, Cardiff
4th Engineer – A. Bains, South Shields
Steward – A. E. Webb
Cook – J. Brown

Peterston – March–July 1928. Voyage 8
Master – G. Clark, Plymouth
Mate – T. D. Edwards, Cardiff
2nd Mate – J. Gould, Pwllheli
Engineer – A. H. Corns, Cardiff
2nd Engineer – G. G. Davies, Cardigan
3rd Engineer – O. James, Hopkinstown
4th Engineer – T. Llewelyn, Glynarthon

Steward – C. Bowen
Cook – J. Lawrence

Ethel Radcliffe – August to October 1906. Voyage 57
Master – T. Wood, Cardiff
Mate – R. R. Gore-Bell, Penarth
2nd Mate – C. A. King, London

Engineer – D. Griffiths, Cardiff
2nd Engineer – E. Davies, Machen
3rd Engineer – A. Ritchie, Cardiff
Steward – R. Ruddock, Bath
Cook – F. T. Marsh

Ethel Radcliffe – August – December 1907. Voyage 62
Master – T. Wood, Cardiff
Mate – J. Williamson, Scarborough
2nd Mate – D. Bertie, Cardiff
Engineer – D. Griffiths. Cardiff
2nd Engineer – P. Fentiman, Abergavenny
3rd Engineer – A. Ritchie, Cardiff
Steward – A. Murphy
Cook – T. Halverson

Ethel Radcliffe – 1920 – 1. Voyage 1
Master – M. Mathias, Cardigan
Mate – J. Davies, Aberarth
2nd Mate – J. H. Jones, Aberarth
3rd Mate – R. A. Gregson, Middlesborough
Engineer – A. E. Richards, Cardiff
2nd Engineer – A. E. Lofthouse, Stockton-on-Tees
3rd Engineer – W. Peters, South Shields
4th Engineer – G. R. Smith, Stockton
Steward – E. Lewis
Cook – F. Grey

Washington – May – August 1907. Voyage 2
Master – M. Mathias, Cardigan
Mate – A. Brinkworth, Gloucester
2nd Mate – A. Gracey, Barry
Engineer – J. Murdoch, Barry
2nd Engineer – A. S. Williams, Cardiff
3rd Engineer – H. L. Winter, Newport
4th Engineer – J. Thomas, Cardiff
Steward – J. Kasilow, Rotterdam
Cook – J. Dubbleman

Washington – April – June 1912. Voyage 22
Master – M. Mathias, Cardigan
Mate – I. Isaac, Newport, Pemb.
2nd Mate – D. J. Morgan, Fishguard
Engineer – J. Murdoch, Barry Dock
2nd Engineer – D. A. Rees, Burry Port

3rd Engineer – H. Doncaster, Jarrow
4th Engineer – L. Knott, South Shields
Steward – A. Stone
Cook – C. Manterson

Anthony Radcliffe – April to June 1906. Voyage 57
Master – W. Thomas, Llaniestyn
Mate – J. S. Mills, Cardiff
2nd Mate – J. Edwards, Cardiff
Engineer – W. J. Powell, Bridgend
2nd Engineer – J. Davies, Machen
3rd Engineer – R. T. Richards, Worcester
Steward – C. L. de Meis, Rotterdam
Cook – J. McDonald

Anthony Radcliffe – 1907–8. Voyage 63
Master – R. Rees, St. Dogmaels
Mate – E. J. Feather, Pontypool
2nd Mate – W. Evans, Anglesey
Engineer – J. Davies, Machen
2nd Engineer – R. A. Jordan, Abergavenny
3rd Engineer – G. R. Jenkins, Llandaff
Steward – J. A. Rausch
Cook – F. Bildan

Llanarth – 1934–3. Voyage 18
Master – J. R. Jenkins, Aber-porth, Cardigan
Mate – J. J. Parry, Sarnau, Cardigan
2nd Mate – Tudor Evans, Porthmadog
3rd Mate – T. G. R. Davies, Kidwelly
Engineer – A. E. Richards, Cardiff
2nd Engineer – C. R. Tudor, Cardigan
3rd Engineer – R. Burris, Cardiff
4th Engineer – M. L. Roberts, Barry
Steward – W. H. Cooper
Cook – W. Jemmett

Clarissa Radcliffe – 1934–5. Voyage 42
Master – E. Jones, Llanarth
Mate – D. L. Davies, Cilgerran
2nd Mate – W. John, Barry
3rd Mate – J. G. Thomas, Ammanford
Engineer – T. L. Bowen, Newcastle Emlyn
2nd Engineer – A. F. Manley, Ilfracombe
3rd Engineer – E. M. James, Penarth

4th Engineer – R. W. Thomas, Cardiff
Steward – J. Young
Cook – T. Thompson

Vera Radcliffe – January – July 1925. Voyage 1
Master – M. Mathias, Cardigan
Mate – T. Jones, Aberarth, Cardigan
2nd Mate – J. M. Shippen, Port Talbot
3rd Mate – W. A. Hancock, Settle, Yorkshire
Engineer – D. J. Rees, Cardiff
2nd Engineer – R. Dent, Cardiff
3rd Engineer – R. Burris, Bedwas
4th Engineer – A. J. Davies, Cardiff
Steward – E. R. Lewis
Cook – R. Brown

Vera Radcliffe – January – July 1929. Voyage 12
Master – J. W. Jones, St. Dogmaels
Mate – Evan Jones, Llanarth
2nd Mate – G. D. Howes, Hull
3rd Mate – D. A. Jenkins, St. Dogmaels
Engineer – D. J. Rees, Cardiff
2nd Engineer – W. Dyer, Cardiff
3rd Engineer – R. Burris, Bedwas
4th Engineer – Glyn Jenkins, Senghenydd
Steward – Evan Rees
Cook – Geo. Wignall

Llanwern – 1028 – 9. Voyage 1
Master – G. Clark, Plymouth
Mate – H. Roberts, St. Dogmaels
2nd Mate – H. Roberts, Morfa Nefyn
3rd Mate – W. Williams, Clydach Vale
Engineer – A. H. Corns, Cardiff
2nd Engineer – D. H. Lynn, Sunderland
3rd Engineer – D. W. Jones, Barry Dock
4th Engineer – A. E. Smith, Sunderland
Steward – C. Bowen
Cook – G. Thompson

Llanwern – September – December 1930. Voyage 8
Master – G. Clark, Plymouth
Mate – H. Roberts, St. Dogmaels
2nd Mate – W. T. Williams, Clydach
3rd Mate – G. H. Wood, Waltham

Engineer – A. H. Corns, Cardiff
2nd Engineer – R. Guinee, Rumney Hill
3rd Engineer – P. Currie, Penarth
4th Engineer – J. D. Evans, Porthcawl
Steward – C. Bowen
Cook – R. P. Soares

Boverton – March–May 1911. Voyage 3
Master – T. Jones, Blaenporth
Mate – A. Hunkin, St. Austell
2nd Mate – R. Williams, Cardiff
Engineer – R. Hughes, Porthmadog
2nd Engineer – L. Trenchard, Cardiff
3rd Engineer – W. Thomas, Cowbridge
Steward – J. A. Slultjen
Cook – P. Noe

Boverton – 1911–12. Voyage 6
Master – J. Jones, Aberarth
Mate – A. Hunkin, St. Austell
2nd Mate – G. Owen, Porthmadog
Engineer – R. Hughes, Porthmadog
2nd Engineer – W. Thomas, Cowbridge
3rd Engineer – E. J. Belton, Cardiff
Steward – E. Cooper
Cook – F. J. Brandt

Wimborne – 1911–12. Voyage 1
Master – E. H. Dolton, Brixham
Mate – W. Williams, Dinas Cross
2nd Mate – A. E. Davies, Newcastle Emlyn
3rd Mate – O. Morris, Porthmadog
Engineer – D. M. Evans, Cardiff
2nd Engineer – H. Edmunds, Machen
3rd Engineer – E. J. Hughes, Dowlais
4th Engineer – F. W. Jones, Machen
Steward – R. Ruddick
Cook – A. James

Wimborne – June–September 1912. Voyage 3
Master – J. Thomas, Cardiff
Mate – W. Williams, Dinas Cross
2nd Mate – A. Nyblad, Newport, Mon.
3rd Mate – W. C. Kirby, Cardiff
Engineer – D. M. Evans, Cardiff

2nd Engineer – H. Edmunds. Machen
3rd Engineer – E. J. Hughes, Dowlais
4th Engineer – F. W. Jones, Machen
Steward – R. Ruddock
Cook – J. Lewis

Wimborne – 1918–19. Voyage 13
Master – J. W. Jones, Cardigan
Mate – T. M. Thomas, Newborough
2nd Mate – Evan Watkins, Porthmadog
3rd Mate – Dd. J. Roberts, Dinas Cross
Engineer – A. E. Richards, Cardiff
2nd Engineer – Geo. F. Ferguson, East Boldon
3rd Engineer – D. A. Harris, Cilgerran
4th Engineer – R. Hobbs, Chepstow

Wimborne – June–November 1923. Voyage 25
Master – R. Roberts, Sarn nr. Pwllheli
Mate – T. Jones, Aberarth
2nd Mate – D. Williams, Corris
3rd Mate – H. Denham, Reading
Engineer – L. C. Thomas, Dinas Powis
2nd Engineer – E. J. Close, Barry
3rd Engineer – G. A. Lewis, Merthyr
4th Engineer – C. G. Dando, Ynysddu
Steward – G. Bonnici
Cook – F. Marian

Flimston – May–September 1925. Voyage 1
Master – S. H. Mathias, Newport, Pembs.
Mate – W. Evans, Cardiff
2nd Mate – A. Haythornthwaite, Plymouth
Engineer – W. Powell, Barry Dock
2nd Engineer – F. Griffiths, Cardiff
3rd Engineer – W. Dunford, Rumney
4th Engineer – R. Pritchard, Nevin
Steward – W. R. Pitt
Cook – J. Millar

Flimston – April–July 1931. Voyage 17
Master – J. A. Davies, Cardigan
Mate – E. O. Jenkins, Aberporth
2nd Mate – G. Evans, Kidwelly
3rd Mate – R. T. Charles, Crewe
Engineer – J. C. West, Penarth

2nd Engineer – W. Owen, Anglesey
3rd Engineer – J. Davies, Cilgerran
4th Engineer – J. Hitchings, Llanelly
Steward – E. R. Lewis
Cook – A. Pierre

Llangorse – July – October 1912. Voyage 49
Master – J. Alexander, Cardiff
Mate – W. B. Davies, Cardiff
2nd Mate – E. Jones, Porthmadog
Engineer – J. R. Abraham, Bristol
2nd Engineer – E. Davies, Caerphilly
3rd Engineer – W. Ballantyne, Cardiff
4th Engineer – C. Lyttleton, St. Fagans
Steward – H. Lewin, St. Fagans
Cook – J. Spoonheimer

Llangorse – 1917 – 1918. Voyage 1
Master – J. Davies, Aberporth
Mate – O. Davies, Llanarth, Cardigan
2nd Mate – T. Thomas, Cardigan
Engineer – W. J. Powell, Barry
2nd Engineer – J. L. Vickery, Llantwit Vardre
3rd Engineer – E. C. Capel, Cardiff
4th Engineer – S. Jones, Sunderland
Steward – H. Gaunt
Cook – W. Maunders, London

Boverton – August—September 1921. Voyage 21
Master – S. H. Mathias, Newport, Pembs.
Mate – S. Jones, Morfa Nevin
2nd Mate – J. Jones, Aberdaron
Engineer – J. E. Davies, Barry
2nd Engineer – R. O. Lazarus, Pentraeth, Anglesey
3rd Engineer – J. Williams, Llandre
Steward – C. Frediksen
Cook – F. S. Green

Boverton – 1925 – 6. Voyage 46
Master – J. James, Aber-porth
Mate – D. G. Evans, New Quay
2nd Mate – J. J. Parry, Sarnau, Cardigan
3rd Mate –
Engineer – R. O. Lazarus, Pentraeth, Anglesey
2nd Engineer – Wm. Davies, Cardigan

3rd Engineer – A. Jones, Blaina
4th Engineer –
Steward – S. O. Hogg
Cook – J. Armstrong

Llandilo – April–August 1928. Voyage 1
Master – T. Jones, Aberarth
Mate – J. Jones, Rhoshirwaun
2nd Mate – E. Jones, Rhymney
3rd Mate – F. Evans, Liverpool
Engineer – E. J. Close, Barry
2nd Engineer – W. Davies, Cardigan
3rd Engineer – A. W. Evans, Cardiff
4th Engineer – T. J. Edwards, Cardiff
Steward – J. Shaw
Cook – A. Hall

Llandilo – 1932–3. Voyage 15
Master – John Jones, Rhoshirwaun
Mate – J. Griffiths, Amlwch
2nd Mate – R. G. Roberts, Llanwnda
3rd Mate – S. Jones, Newcastle Emlyn
Engineer – E. J. Close, Barry
2nd Engineer – D. G. Williams
3rd Engineer – D. O. Jones, Cardiff
4th Engineer – R. M. Locke, Newport
Steward – R. H. Evans
Cook – L. P. Clarke

Catherine Radcliffe – March–September 1925. Voyage 1
Master – John Davies, Llangrannog
Mate – W. G. James, Cardiff
2nd Mate – W. R. Burgess, Lynmouth
3rd Mate – H. Neale, Swanage
Engineer – L. C. Thomas, Dinas Powis
2nd Engineer – F. Conroy, Cardiff
3rd Engineer – J. W. Fowler and T. R. Williams, Cardiff
4th Engineer – C. Proctor, Middlesborough
Steward – J. Lindsay
Cook – N. McGhee

Catherine Radcliffe – June–July 1929. Voyage 12
Master – T. Owens, Llangrannog
Mate – W. G. James, Cardiff
2nd Mate – H. Jones, Nevin

3rd Mate – J. Jones, Newcastle Emlyn
Engineer – G. H. Davids, Cardiff
2nd Engineer – A. Outhwaite, Cadoxton
3rd Engineer – J. Hughes, Penrhyndeudraeth
4th Engineer – W. J. Harrington, Cardiff
Steward – W. H. Slocombe
Cook – W. F. Macauley

Llanfair – June–September 1928. Voyage 1
Master – S. H. Mathias, Newport, Pembs.
Mate – J. E. Thomas, Newcastle Emlyn
2nd Mate – D. O. Jenkins, Tresaith, Cardigan
3rd Mate – T. Evans, Porthmadog
Engineer – W. Powell, Barry
2nd Engineer – D. J. Harries, New Quay, Cardigan
3rd Engineer – G. Robinson, South Shields
4th Engineer – F. E. Billot, Cardiff
Steward – E. Medland
Cook – L. Clarke

Llanfair – 1929–30. Voyage 7
Master – S. H. Mathias, Newport, Pembs.
Mate – J. E. Thomas, Newcastle Emlyn
2nd Mate – R. E. Worley, Porthmadog
3rd Mate – J. G. Morris, Borthygest, Porthmadog
Engineer – R. Dent, Cardiff
2nd Engineer – D. J. Harries, New Quay, Cardigan
3rd Engineer – F. E. Billot, Cardiff
4th Engineer – A. J. Gibby, Milford Haven
Steward – E. A. Medland
Cook – R. P. Suares

The Second World War

The Second World War was as disastrous for Evan Thomas Radcliffe as the first for an appreciable proportion of the fleet was lost. No fewer than 11 vessels were sunk:

1940	27 June	*Llanarth* – torpedoed off Lands End 47.30°N 10.30°W on voyage from Melbourne with flour.
	11 August	*Llanfair* – torpedoed on a voyage from Mackay and Bowen (Queensland) to U.K. with sugar 54.48°N 13.46°W.
	23 August	*Llanishen* – bombed and sunk SE of Wick 58.17°N 2.27°W on voyage from Three Rivers (Quebec) to Leith with maize.
1941	26 February	*Llanwern* – Bombed by aircraft off south west coast of Ireland. 54.67°N 17.06°W on voyage from Sorel (Quebec) with grain and timber for Avonmouth.
	17 April	*Ethel Radcliffe* – Torpedoed by E. Boat off East Anglian coast on a voyage from St. John's New Brunswick to Yarmouth with maize. Beached on Yarmouth sands, but bombed and made total loss on 14 May 1941.
1942	12 May	*Llanover* – torpedoed in North Atlantic 52.50°N 29.04°W on voyage from New York and Halifax, Nova Scotia for London with wheat, apples and tanks.
	2 November	*Llandilo* – torpedoed south of St. Helena on voyage from New York. 27.03°S 02.59°W.
1943	17 February	*Llanashe* – torpedoed off Port Elizabeth 34.00°S 28.30°E on voyage from New York.
	10 March	*Clarissa Radcliffe* – torpedoed with loss of all hands, 42.00°N 62.00°W on voyage from Pepel with iron ore.
	30 May	*Llancarfan* – bombed and sunk 2 miles south of St. Vincent while on a voyage from Glasgow to Lisbon and Melitta with coal and coke.

1944 30 March *Vera Radcliffe* – handed over to the Ministry of War Transport for use as a blockship on Normandy beaches.

This left the company with a greatly depleted fleet, for only 5 vessels came through the war unscathed. They were *Llanberis, Llangollen, Peterston, Flimston* and *Llandaff.* British ships were being lost much faster than they could possibly be replaced and the Government decided that it would be impossible to back a new shipbuilding programme entirely in this country which was so vulnerable to enemy attack. With this in mind a British Merchant Shipbuilding Mission left for the U.S.A. in September 1940 and the terms of their brief was *to endeavour to obtain at the earliest possible moment the delivery of merchant tonnage . . . of vessels of the tramp type of about 10,000 tons deadweight.*[17] A total of 354 'Fort type' vessels were also delivered from Canadian yards in addition to the 'Ocean' and 'Liberty' ships obtained from U.S. yards. Radcliffes obtained 6 of these vessels together with the *Samskern* a vessel lent to the Ministry of War Transport under the Lease-Lend system at a charter rate of a dollar a year.

With the great depletion in the fleet as the result of the war, the company was forced to look elsewhere for extra tonnage. American and Canadian standard vessels of the 'Fort' type were obtained. They were:

Fort Rupert (4262 GRT) 424′ × 57′ × 37′6″
Built by the Grand Trunk Pacific Development Company Ltd., Prince Rupert, British Colombia in 1942. Managed by ETR on behalf of the Ministry of War Transport from 5 January 1943.

Fort Remy (4240 GRT) 424′ × 57′ × 37.5′
Built by United Shipyards Ltd., Montreal, Quebec in 1942. Managed by ETR from 3 March 1943.

P.L.M. 17 (2076 GRT) 345′ × 49′ × 27′
A French vessel built in 1922 by Smith Duck & Co. Ltd., Middlesborough. Managed on behalf of the Ministry of War Transport from 21 March 1943.

Fort le Traite (4243 GRT) 424.5′ × 57′ × 37.5′
Built in 1942 by West Coast Shipbuilders Ltd., Vancouver, British Columbia. Managed by ETR from 1 June 1943.

Fort Saleesh (4252 GRT) 424.5′ × 57′ × 37.5′
Built 1943 by North Vancouver Ship Repair Ltd., Vancouver, British Columbia. Managed by ETR from 18 February 1944.

Fort Richelieu (4227 GRT) 424.7′ × 57′ × 37.5′
Built 1943 by Marine Industries Ltd., Sorel, Quebec. Managed by ETR from 7 January 1944.

Samskern (4388 GRT) 423′ × 57′ × 34′
Built 1944 by Bethlehem Fairfield Shipyard, Baltimore, Maryland. Managed by ETR from 3 November 1944.

Fort Miami (4243 GRT) 424.6′ × 57.2′ × 37.5′
Built by North Vancouver Ship Repair Ltd., 1942. Managed by ETR from 1 January 1945.

The period after 1945 was a period of reconstruction and rebuilding, although Evan Thomas Radcliffe, in common with all other South Wales shipowners, was never to enjoy the prosperity of the pre first World War period. Cardiff was to witness a gradual decline in the fortunes of its docks as the export of coal diminished, for Cardiff, above all, was a coal exporting port and its fortunes had been built on the export of that one single commodity. Many of the Cardiff tramp steamers were concerned in the coal trade and the vessels owned by Radcliffes were principally designed for transporting coal. The company, therefore, had to look elsewhere for its freight and with the change of ownership to the Evans and Reid group, as a fully integrated company within the group after some years in partnership with Evans and Reid, the Radcliffe fleet was principally an oil tanker fleet.

In 1946 the company possessed only 5 ships of its own: *Llanberis* (built 1928); *Llangollen* (built 1928); *Peterston* (built 1925); *Flimston* (built 1925) and *Llandaff* (built 1937).

It was operating another eight standard vessels on behalf of the Ministry of Transport or on charter. They were: *Empire Eddystone* (built 1947); *Empire Prospect* (built 1945); *Fort Richelieu* (built 1943); *Fort Saltash* (built 1943); *Fort Le Traite* (built 1942); *Fort Remy* (built 1942); *Fort Rupert* (built 1942); *Samskern* (built 1942).

By 1949 the *Peterston* and *Flimston* had been sold, the standard vessels had been handed back and in the rebuilding of the company a number of second-hand vessels were obtained. They were:

Llanishen 1944

Llanishen – a tanker of 6408 tons built as the *Rye Court* in 1945 by Pennsylvania Sun Shipbuilding and Drydock Company, Chato, Pennsylvania for an American owner. Purchased 24 November, 1947.

Llanarth – a tanker of 4826 tons built in 1944 by J. A. Jones Construction CO. Inc., Brunswick, Georgia, U.S.A. as the *Helmspey* for the Strath Steamship Company, Empire House, Mountstuart Square, Cardiff. Purchased by Radcliffe's, 12 July 1947.

Llanwern – a ship of 4993 tons built in 1937 as the *Nailsea Moor* for the Nailsea S.S. Co. of Cardiff by Bartram of Sunderland. Purchased by Radcliffe's 25 May 1949.

In 1949 the fleet consisted of: *Llanberis* (1928); *Llangollen* (1928); *Llanishen* (1945); *Llanarth* (1931); *Llanover* (1944) and *Llandaff* (1937).

In addition the *Granton Glen,* a vessel built in 1918 and owned by the Culliford Shipping Company of Cardiff, in liquidation was taken over for a year in 1948–9.

The pattern of trading had changed considerably; the tankers were of course mainly concerned with the carriage of oil from the Persian Gulf, Sumatra and elsewhere to European ports, but the other steamers – the *Llanover* and *Llanwern* were concerned with world-wide tramping, rarely visiting their home port of Cardiff.

In October 1949 when the *Helmspey*'s name was changed to *Llanover* the vessel undertook the following voyages:

Voyage 7.

December 16, 1949.	Left Swansea for Melbourne and Sydney.
January 27, 1950.	Arrived Melbourne.
February 10, 1950.	Arrived Sydney.
March 15, 1950.	Left Sydney for South Africa.
April 13, 1950.	Arrived East London.
April 14, 1950.	Arrived Lourenço Marques.
April 27, 1950.	Left Lourenço Marques for Melbourne.
May 21, 1950.	Arrived Melbourne.
July 5, 1950.	Left Melbourne for Alexandria.
August 12, 1950.	Arrived Alexandria.
August 22, 1950.	Left Alexandria for Bonn.
August 28, 1950.	Left Bonn for Middlesborough.
September 15, 1950.	Left Middlesborough for West Hartlepool (Dry Dock).
October 11th 1950.	Left West Hartlepool for London.

Voyage 8 took the vessel to Dar-es-Salaam, Lourenço Marques, Melbourne, Geelong, Naples, Cagliari, Singapore, Yokohama, Vancouver and Djibouti where on 19 March 1951 the vessel was handed over to its new owners, the Liberian Shipping Inc. of Monrovia.

The *Nailsea Moor* renamed *Llanwern*, on 18 June 1949 also sailed world-wide. Voyage 3 for example:

June 20, 1949.	Left Middlesborough for London.
July 3, 1949.	Sailed London to Freetown, Accra and Takoradi.
August 12, 1949.	Sailed Accra for Port Harcourt.
September 26, 1949.	Left Takoradi for Las Palmas.
October 7, 1949.	Left Las Palmas for London. (Arrived October 15).

The next voyage was also concerned with West Africa while the fifth voyage sailed a round-the-world voyage to Aden, Sydney, Brisbane, Suva, Vancouver, San Francisco, San Pedro, Belfast, Jarrow-on-Tyne and Glasgow. The vessel was sold at the end of its Far East eighth voyage to Invi Kisen Kabushiki Kaisha of Kobe, Japan and was handed over to its new owners on 21st September 1951.

In 1950 and 1951 too, the *Llandaff* and *Llangollen* of pre-war vintage were disposed of which left the company with one vessel only, the tanker *Llanishen* of 1945 with a new motor vessel, the *Llantrisant*, a freighter of 6140 tons building at Bartram's yard in Sunderland. The vessel was launched on 27th March 1952 and delivered to its owners on 5th September 1952. This vessel was destined to remain in the fleet for only five years for in 1957 she was sold to a Vancouver Company as the *Lake Burnaby.* While she was a Radcliffe vessel, the *Llantrisant* was concerned with world-wide tramping. The voyages she undertook being the following:

Voyage 1 – Sunderland, Oran, Bougie, Liverpool.

Voyage 2 – Liverpool, New Orleans, Balboa, Kobe, Shimizu, Melbourne, Naples, Antwerp.

Voyage 3 – Antwerp, Curacao, Cristobal, Wellington, Dunedin, Adelaide, Karachi, Geelong, Melbourne, London.

Voyage 4 – London, Rosario, Buenos Aires, Antwerp, Hull.

Voyage 5 – Hull, Kassa (West Africa), Newport (Mon.).

Voyage 6 – Newport, Kassa, Quebec, Halifax (Nova Scotia), Avonmouth, Newport, Swansea, Manchester.

Voyage 7 – Manchester, Glasgow, Copenhagen, Trinidad, Quebec, Manchester.

Voyage 8 – Manchester, Montreal, Santiago de Cuba, Kingston (Jamaica), Los Angeles, Vancouver, Seattle, Quebec, Philadelphia, San Francisco, Quebec, Swansea, Rotterdam.

Voyage 9 – Rotterdam, Georgetown, New York, Baltimore, Antwerp, Mobile, Bremen, St. Johns (New Brunswick), Avonmouth, Paramaribo, Quebec, Kingston, Vancouver, San Francisco, Montreal, Cristobal, Portland, Yokohama, Vancouver, Yohohama, Seattle, Tokyo, Suez, Hamburg, Hull.

Llandaff 1953

Hamilton 1960

Llanwern 1962

Since the company in the early fifties had few ships, a number were chartered. Following the delivery of the *Llantrisant* in 1952, another new vessel, the oil tanker *Llandaff* was built by Lithgow's of Glasgow. She remained in the fleet until

1960, for much of the time being chartered to the Anglo-Saxon Petroleum Company Ltd. but on 16th February 1960 she was sold to the Island Shipping Company of Bermuda.

In 1957 a new motor vessel, the freighter *Llantrisant* was delivered by Bartram's of Sunderland while in the following year the oil tanker *Llanishen* was delivered from Swan Hunters yard at Wallsend-on-Tyne. In 1960 the tanker *Hamilton*, built at Tamise, Belgium, was delivered on time charter and the tanker *Llangorse* built by the Furness Shipbuilding Company of Haverton Hill was delivered. In October 1962 the freighter *Llanwern* was delivered by Bartrams of Sunderland.

In 1964 – 5 therefore, the Radcliffe fleet consisted of five vessels: *Llanishen* (1958), *Llantrisant* (1957), *Hamilton* (1960), *Llangorse* (1960) and the *Llanwern* (1962). By 1970 the *Llanwern* and the *Llantrisant* had been sold and in 1971 the last vessel to be built especially for the company the *Stolt Llandaff* was delivered by S.A. Boelwerf of Tamise Belgium. She was a specialised oil and chemical tanker and remained as a Radcliffe vessel on charter to the company from the Stolt Corporation of Monrovia until December 1981. With the sale of the *Hamilton, Llangorse* and *Llanishen,* the *Stolt Llandaff* was to remain the sole vessel in the fleet until 1980 when two small coastal vessels – the *Radcliffe Trader* and the *Radcliffe Venturer* were purchased.

Radcliffe Trader and Radcliffe Venturer

The rise of Evan Thomas Radcliffe and Company as shipowners symbolised the development of Cardiff as one of the principal tramp-ship owning ports of Britain. The company came into being and developed when coal, the principal commodity exported from Cardiff was in world-wide demand and the history of the company, especially before the first world war was the story of enterprise and growth. No wonder that Henry Radcliffe, when he died in 1921 left a fortune of over £1¼ million, for Cardiff 'the coal metropolis of the world' was a 'city of millionaires'; its prosperity being based almost entirely on the export of coal from the South Wales valleys.

Evan Thomas Radcliffe Ships

Aden 1908 (GRT 2482) 313.5 × 43.8 × 13.3
b. 1905 W. Rodgers & Co., Port Glasgow as *Craigmore* for Craig Line S.G.Co.
Purchased by ETR in 1908
1915 – sold to Colonial Coal & Shipping Co. as *Thysa*: renamed *Kostis*
1934 – sold as *Azbassein*
1936 – sold to USSR as *Georgi Dimitrov*

Alex 1914 (GRT 3907) 380 × 51.5 × 22.1
Built by J. Priestland, Sunderland.
built as *Constantinos XII;* then *Ionia*, then *Nicos*
Purchased by ETR in 1938 and named *Alex*
1943 – sold to S. Casteli & Co. – no change of name
1946 – renamed *Noemi*
5 June 1958 – scrapped at Split.

Alma 1896 (GRT 2863)
Built by J. Priestland, Sunderland. Managed on behalf of Shipping Controller 1919-26

Anne Thomas 1882 (GRT 1418) 260 × 35.3 × 17.8
Built by Palmers of Jarrow
Sold Grogstad & Co., Norway – *Lord*

Anthony Radcliffe 1893 (GRT 2865) 315 × 42 × 20′11″
Built by Palmers Co. Ltd., Newcastle.
1908 – renamed *Bonvilston*
Attacked three times in 1916 and 1917 and was finally sunk by torpedo 17 October 1918, 9½ miles NW by W of Corsewall Point.

Asgard 1906 (GRT 4181) 360 × 48 × 20
Built by Northumberland Shipbuilding Co. Ltd. Managed on behalf of Shipping Controller 1919-20

Badminton 1910
See *Llanberis* 1890

Badminton 1912
See *Swindon* 1899

Bala 1884 (GRT 2013) 280 × 35.7 × 20.1
Built by William Gray & Co., West Hartlepool
Sold in December 1903 to the Glanhowny S.S. Co. (Bartlett & Owen) as the *Glanhowny*. Like Evan Thomas, Capt. Thomas Owen was a native of Aberporth, Dyfed and H.A. Bartlett was a Cardiff businessman. The vessel was sold for £8750 and sailed under the command of Thomas Owen, who died aboard the vessel on her third voyage to the Black Sea.

Bala 1907
See *Ethel Radcliffe* 1894

Balingdale (Managed Vessel) 1949
Purchased Societo al Navigazione Tomei, Genoa, 29 April 1949.

Bonvilston 1908
See *Anthony Radcliffe* 1893

Boverton 1910 (GRT 2958) 325 × 46 × 23.4
Built by John Blumer & Co., North Dock, Sunderland for £26,500
3 May 1928 – name changed to *Llangorse*
20 February 1930 – sold to Tallinn Shipping Co. of Esthonia for £17,244 – *Maret*
1941 – USSR named *Sysonby*
28 September 1951 – Broken up.

Catherine Radcliffe 1925 (GRT 5589) 415 × 55 × 28
Built by Craig, Taylor & Co., Stockton-on-Tees. Cost £99,439
23 February 1935. Abandoned after stranding off coast of Japan (Master – T. Owens, Aber-porth, Dyfed) Insured for £70,868

Clarissa Radcliffe 1889 (GRT 2544) 296 × 40.2 × 20.6
Built by Palmers of Jarrow
On a voyage from Odessa to Rotterdam with a cargo of grain, the vessel met a gale off Cape St. Vincent on 30 December 1897. The cargo shifted and the vessel sank with the loss of 16 lives.

Clarrisa Radcliffe 1904 (GRT 4703) 351.5 × 53.1 × 27.6
Built Ropner, Stockton (Yard No. 410) A trunk-decked vessel.
Renamed *Llanover* 1913, *Llangorse* 1917.
1926 – Sold to Watts, Watts & Co. as *Laleham* for £17,758
1926 – Sold to A.A. Kyrtaras, Andros as *Marionga D. Thermiotis*

1947 – Sold to Cia de Nav. Ponanza Ltd., Panama – *Antonios K.*
25 May 1952 – scrapped at Milford Haven.

Clarissa Radcliffe 1913
See *W.I. Radcliffe* 1917

Clarissa Radcliffe 1917 (GRT 6042) 415 × 55.5 × 28.7
Built by Craig Taylor & Co., Stockton-on-Tees in 1915 as the *Windsor.* Cost £251,000
Renamed *Gwent* in 1916 and *Clarissa Radcliffe* in 1917.
On 5 March 1943 the ship left New York for Barrow-in-Furness with a crew of 41 and 10 gunners. She was never heard of again and was presumably torpedoed on 10 March 1943 in Lat 42°N Long 62°W.

Douglas Hill 1890 (GRT 2171) 285 × 37.8 × 20
Built by Palmers Co. Ltd., Newcastle
March 1908 – name changed to *Iolo*
August 1909 – sold to Frederick Childs – *Selworthy*
Lost March 1910.

Dunraven 1896 (GRT 3333) 338 × 46 × 27
Built by Ropner of Stockton-on-Tees, launched 2 October 1896.
The name of the vessel was changed to *Sarah Radcliffe* on delivery of a new *Dunraven* in 1910.
Sunk 11 November 1916 by submarine 170 miles S.W. of Ushant.

Dunraven 1910 (GRT 3117) 341 × 48 × 24′41½″
Built by Tyne Iron Shipbuilding Co. Willington Quay on Tyne.
1917 – Transferred to Royal Navy as Q. ship
10 August 1917 – sunk by torpedo and guns in Bay of Biscay.

Empire Eddystone (Managed Vessel) 1945 (GRT 7318 431 × 56 × 38
Built by W. Gray, West Hartlepool

Empire Prospect (Managed Vessel) 1945 (GRT 7331) 431 × 38 × 38
Built by Walker Shipyard, Newcastle-upon-Tyne.

Ethel Radcliffe 1920 (GRT 5673) 415 × 55 × 28.9
Built by Craig Taylor & Co., Stockton-on-Tees. Cost £274,019
17 April 1941. Damaged by E-boat and put into port at Great Yarmouth.
The vessel was bombed and sunk at that port on 16 May 1941.

Euston 1898 (GRT 2728) 330 × 44 × 24.3
Built by Ropner & Son, Stockton-on-Tees. Delivered 19 July 1898
1910 – name changed to *Gileston*
1926 – sold to Greek owners for £8400 as *Haralampos P.*
1929 sold to W.G. Walton, Cyprian Shipping Co. Ltd. as *Danubian*
18 February 1954 – stranded in fog off Kilyos in Black Sea on voyage in ballast from Alexandria to Constanza;

Euston 1910 (GRT 2841) 325 × 26.6 × 23′3½″
Built by John Blumer & Co., North Dock, Sunderland.
28 October 1917 – torpedoed 35 miles SW of Cape Matapan.

Flimston 1916 (GRT 5751) 415 × 55.5 × 26.7
Built by Craig Taylor & Co., Stockton-on-Tees.
18 December 1916 – captured and bombed by submarine 21 miles NE by E from Ushant.

Flimston 1925 (GRT 4674) 385 × 52 × 26
Built by Bartram, South Dock, Sunderland.
1948 – sold to Woodham S.S. Co. Cardiff as *Woodham Rover*
1950 – sold to Schulte & Bruns as *Konsul Schulte*
14 January 1960 scrapped at Tamise.

Fort La Traite (Managed Vessel) 1942 (GRT 7134) 424 × 57 × 37.5
Built by West Coast Shipbuilding, Vancouver.

Fort Miami (Managed Vessel) 1942 (GRT 7134) 424 × 57.2 × 37.5
Built by Vancouver Ship Repairers Ltd., Vancouver.

Fort Richelieu (Managed Vessel) 1943 (GRT 7150) 424 × 57.2 × 37.5
Built by Marine Industries Ltd., Soull, Quebec.

Fort Remy (Managed Vessel) 1942 (GRT 7127) 424 × 57 × 37.5
Built by United Shipyards Ltd., Montreal
In fleet 1942-49

Fort Rupert (Managed Vessel) 1942 (GRT 7141) 424 × 57 × 37.6
Built by Grand Trunk Pacific Development Co. Ltd. Prince Rupert, British Columbia.
In fleet 1946-49

Fort Saleesh (Managed Vessel) 1943 (GRT 7167) 424 × 57.2 × 37.5
Built by North Vancouver Shiprepairers Ltd.

Gileston 1910
See *Euston* 1898

Granton Glen 1918 (GRT 2485) 257 × 43.8 × 20
Built by Manitoba S.B.Co., Wis. ex. Catherine, Stratford, Lake Greenwood. Owned by Culliford Shipping Co. Ltd., liquidated 1947, management of vessel taken over by ETR for 1 year.

Gwenllian Thomas 1882 (GRT 1082) 233 × 31.2 × 17
Built by Palmer's Shipbuilding and Iron Co., Jarrow-on-Tyne.
Delivered Cardiff 24/6/1882 and sailed with a cargo of coal for St. Nazaire, returning to Cardiff with iron ore from Bilbao. She was commanded by Capt. Evan Thomas.
Sold December 1905 as *Richard*

Gwent 1909 (GRT 3344 330 × 48 × 23
Built 1901 as *Evangeline* by R. Thomson, Sunderland
Purchased from Anglo-Grecian S.S. Co. 1909 for £17,350
1912 – sold for £22,589 to London-Piraeus S.S. Co. *Sain Dimitrios*
2 March 1918 – sunk

Gwent 1916
See *Clarissa Radcliffe* 1917

Hamilton 1960 (GRT 13,186) 560 × 72 × 30.9
Tanker built by C. Boel et Fils, Tamise, Belgium.
Launched 28 January 1960. Still in service as *Feoso Sun.*

Hanley 1902 (GRT 3331) 326 × 48 × 23
Built by Joseph L. Thompson & Son, Sunderland, for Woodruff Shillito & Co., Cardiff in 1902. Purchased immediately by Radcliffe
April 1912 – sold to Tom Lewis & Co.,
30 May 1917 – sunk off Irish coast by torpedo, 95 miles west of Bishops Rock – 1 life lost.

Helemar 1957 (GRT 544) 187 × 29 × 12
Charter by ETR 6 March 1957 (Owners Velmont S.S. Co.)
Sold to Pieter Hougerverff, Deest (Holland) 23 July 1958
Still sailing as *Hamnfiord*

Helmpeg
See *Llanover* 1949

High Park (Managed Vessel) 1943 (GRT 7143) 424 × 57 × 37
Built by Davie Shipbuilding, Lauzon-Levis, Quebec.

Iolo 1910
See *Sarah Radcliffe* 1889

Iolo 1913
See *Douglas Hill* 1890

Iolo 1913
See *Paddington* 1898

Iolo 1917
See *Llanover* 1899

Iolo Morgannwg 1882 (GRT 1241) 251 × 33.25 × 18′
Built by Palmers of Jarrow
Sold December 1905 as *Pontus,* later *Held* (Swedish flag)

Jane Radcliffe 1890 (GRT 1830) 271 × 37 × 18
Built by Ropner, Stockton-on-Tees
August 1911 – sold to Otto Weens of Malmo, named *Hjalma*

Jane Radcliffe 1911
See *Windsor* 1897

Kate Thomas 1884 (GRT 1557) 269 × 36.4 × 18
Built by Palmers of Jarrow
Lost near Ceuta 21 October 1895 on voyage from Cardiff to Brindisi with coal.

Lady Palmer 1889 (GRT 2752) 322 × 40 × 24
Built by Palmers of Jarrow for Hall Bros., Newcastle
Chartered by Daniel Radcliffe 1890-91
Sunk in Dover Straits 1891.

Llanberis 1890 (GRT 2269) 290 × 38 × 22.4
Built by Ropner, Stockton-on-Tees for £34,000
Jan 1910 – name changed to *Badminton*

Feb. 10th 1912 – sold for £8,500 to Coroniadis Bros. – *Coroniadis*
1914 – sold as *Malgas*
1916 – sold as *Georgios Markettos*

Llanberis 1910
See *Llandudno* 1897

Llanberis 1928 (GRT 5055) 400 × 53 × 28
Built by Hawthorn Leslie & Co., Wallsend-on-Tyne for £86,573
Launched 12 October 1927
1950 (17 February) sold to Basil J. Mauros, Piraeus as *Theoskepasti*
1956 – sold as *Valente*

Llancarvan 1917
See *W.I. Radcliffe* 1904

Llancarfan 1937 (GRT 4910) 401 × 53 × 26.6
Built by White's Marine Engineering, Hebburn-on-Tyne as *Biddlestone* for White Shipping Co., Newcastle.
1940 – Purchased and renamed *Llancarfan.*
30 May 1943 – Bombed and sunk 2 miles south of St. Vincent.

Llandaff 1937 (GRT 4826) 417 × 56 × 251
Built Bartram, Sunderland.
First voyage to Port Said – Poti – Baltimore under the command of J.R. Jenkins, Aber-porth, Dyfed.
1 October 1951 – sold to K.G. Bornhofen of Hamburg as *Max Bornhofen*
1959 – sold to Greek owners as *Pilastassios*
Ran aground Esbjerg Roads 20 February 1959, refloated 7 March 1959.
Scrapped at Ghent 10 September 1959.

Llandaff 1953 (GRT 12501) 556 × 73 × 31
Built at Lithgow's of Glasgow. Launched 26 January 1952
17 February 1960 – sold to Island Shipping Co., Bermuda as *Wheat King.*

Llandilo 1928 (GRT 4966) 400 × 53 × 26
Built by Bartram & Sons, Sunderland. Delivered 6 February 1928. Maiden voyage Tyne – Algiers (Coal) – Rosarro – La Plata – Hamburg (grain) under the command of T. Jones, Aberarth, Dyfed. (*Twm Cadno*)
2 November 1942 Torpedoed south of St. Helier in position
27° 03S × 02° 59′W

Llandrindod 1900 (GRT 3841) 351 × 48 × 28.4
Built by Richardson, Duck & Co., Stockton
18 May 1917 – sunk by torpedo 165 miles NW by W of Fastnet.

Llandudno 1897 (GRT 4074) 350 × 46.6 × 27.3
Built by Ropner & Son, Stockton-on-Tees. Delivered 26 July 1897
1910 – renamed *Llanberis*
1927 – sold to Richards, Longstaff & Co., London as *Yorkminster.*

Llandudno 1910 (GRT 4186) 362 × 50 × 27
Built by Tyne Iron Shipbuilding Co., Willington Quay-on-Tyne.
1 August 1917 – Captured and sunk by submarine 110 miles SW of Porquerolles Island, Gulf of Lyons. 1 lost life.

Llanfair 1928 (GRT 4966) 400 × 53.4 × 26
Built by Bartram & Sons, Sunderland.
Maiden voyage to Port Said with coal, Cuba to Liverpool with sugar (Master Samuel H. Mathias, Newport, Pembrokeshire)
11 October 1940 – torpedoed 54.48N by 13.46W.

Llangollen 1900 (GRT 3842) 351 × 48 × 28.4
Built by Richardson, Duck & Co., Stockton-on-Tees. Cost £49,371
Sold 4 October 1926 to Greece as *Issidoro* for £13,500. The vessel completed 81 voyages for Radcliffes.

Llangollen 1928 (GRT 5055) 400 × 53 × 26
Built by Hawthorn Leslie & Co., Wallsend-on-Tyne Cost £86,990
(1st Master – D.G. Evans, New Quay, Dyfed).
8 February 1950 – sold to Nicholas a Simbouras, Athens, as *Aretis*
1952 – sold as *Maria Christina*
1960 – sold as *Kettara II*
7 February 1960 – scrapped at Nagoya.

Llangorse 1900 (GRT 3841) 351 × 48 × 28.4
Built by Richardson, Duck & Co., Stockton-on-Tees. Cost £45,114
8 September 1916 – torpedoed 48 miles WSW of Cape Matapan. Insured for £120,450.

Llangorse 1917
See *Clarissa Radcliffe* 1904

Llangorse 1928
See *Boverton* 1910

Llangorse 1960 (GRT 21,840)
Tanker built, Furness Shipbuilding Co., Haverton Hill. Delivered August 1960. In fleet until c.1966

Llanishen 1929 (GRT 3836) 340 × 48 × 26
Built by Richardson Duck & Co., Stockton-on-Tees
9 August 1917 – torpedoed and beached 8 miles N by E of Cape of Crevs, Gulf of Lyons. Total loss.

Llanishen 1929 (GRT 5052) 400 × 54 × 25.9
Built by Bartram, Sunderland for £82,568. Delivered 29 April 1929 and left on maiden voyage from the Tyne to Santos with coal (Master R. Roberts, Aberdovey, Gwynedd)
23 October 1941 – Bombed and sunk south east of Wick. 58.17N by 02.27W.

Llanishen 1944 (GRT 10,735) 506 × 68 × 39
Tanker built as *Rye Cove.* Purchased from Ministry of War Transport in 1947.
31 May 1956 – sold to Panama as *Anna O.*
25 December 1962 – arrived Castellon, Spain for scrapping.

Llanishen 1957 (GRT 20,976) 635 × 64 × 34
Tanker built Swan Hunter & Wigham Richardson, Wallsend-on-Tyne
Delivered 17 January 1958. Still sailing as *Petrola 19.*

Llanover 1899 (GRT 3840) 351 × 48 × 28.4
Built by Richardson, Duck & Co., Stockton-on-Tees
Renamed *Paddington* February 1913
Renamed *Iolo* February 1917
Torpedoed and sunk 42 miles SW of Fastnet 17 February 1917. 2 dead. Master, Chief Engineer and 2 gunners made prisoner.

Llanover 1913
See *Clarissa Radcliffe* 1904

Llanover 1917 (GRT 4240) 390 × 53 × 23
Built by Pickersgill, Sunderland

1917 – sold to Johnston Line as *Linmore*
1920 – sold to Dr. T.G. Adams as *Shannonmede*
1924 – sold to Edw. Nichol & Co. as *Littleton*
1932 – sold to Heirs of L.Z. Cambanis, Andros as *Leonidas Z. Cambanis*
3 April 1941 – torpedoed SE of Cape Farewell.

Llanover 1928 (GRT 4959) 400 × 53 × 26.
Built by Bartram, Sunderland (Launched 4 November 1927) Master John James. Aberporth, Dyfed.
12 May 1942 – torpedoed North Atlantic 52.50N by 29.04W.

Llanover 1944 (GRT 7281) 424 × 57 × 35
Built at Brunswick, Georgia, USA by J.A. Jones Construction Inc. as *Samlorian* and sold in 1944 to Strath S.S. Co. of Cardiff as *Helmspey.*
27 October 1949 – Purchased by ETR – renamed *Llanover.*
19 November 1951 – sold to Liberian Shipping Inc as *Capestar*
1960 – Resold as *Athlos*

Llantrisant 1952 (GRT 6140) 460 × 62 × 30
Motor vessel built by Bartram, Sunderland. Delivered 5 September 1952
1957 – sold to Western Canadian S.S. Co., Vancouver as *Lake Burnaby*
3 November 1958 – stranded on Bancorran Reef, Phillipines – total loss.

Llantrisant 1957 (GRT 6171) Motor Vessel 477.6 × 62 × 30.8
Built by Bartram, Sunderland. Delivered March 1958.
Transferred to Elenmaris Corp. Piraeus as *Eleni M*

Llanwern 1928 (GRT 4966) 400 × 53 × 26
Built by Bartram, Sunderland (launched 1 September 1928)
Maiden voyage to Cardiff – Santos (coal) – Rosario – Buenos Aires – Avonmouth (grain and wheat). Master G. Clark, Plymouth.
26 February 1941 – bombed and sunk west of Ireland in position 54.67N by 17.06W.

Llanwern 1937 (GRT 4993) 420 × 56 × 28
Built as *Nailsea Moor* for Nailsea S.S. Co. by Bartram of Sunderland.
Purchased by ETR 11 June 1949, renamed *Llanwern*
21 September 1957 Sold to Inui Kisen Kabushlui of Kobe, Japan as *Kenkon Maru.*
1961 – resold as *Fujisan Maru* (to become fish factory)

Llanwern 1962 (GRT 9229 498 × 61′11″ × 26′11¼″
Built by Bartram, Sunderland (launched 19 July 1962)
Renamed *Captain Michael* Later *Agios Penteleimon.*

Manchester 1890 (GRT 2072) 285 × 37.2 × 20
Built by William Gray & Co., West Hartlepool.
February 1912 – sold to Artaza & Co., Bilbao – *Arcotis* later *L.C. Stensland; Hitteroy Browton* and lastly as the Russian *Voikov.*

Maria N. Roussos 1909 (GRT 3129) 346 × 50 × 23
Built by William Gray of Hartlepool
Chartered from 28 July 1925 to 21 November 1929

Mary Thomas 1889 (GRT 2159) 275.5 × 37.8 × 20.1
Built by Palmers & Co., Newcastle upon Tyne
May 1908 – sold to the Glanhowny Steamship Company (H.A. Bartlett) as *Barto*
October 1909 – sold to Samuel Rowe as *Jane Rowe*

Novasli 1920 (GRT 3204) 342.2 × 48 × 21.9
Built by R. Thompson & Sons, Sunderland
Norwegian vessel owned by A. Skibs.
Chartered from Ministry of War Transport 1941-46

Paddington 1898 (GRT 3903) 350 × 46.6 × 27.3
Built by Ropner & Sons, Stockton-on-Tees.
Name changed to *Iolo* March 1913
11 October 1916 – sunk by submarine 153 miles N of Vardo, off north coast of Norway.

Paddington 1913
See *Llanover* 1899

Paddington 1917
See *Patagonia* 1906

Patagonia 1906 (GRT 5084) 392 × 50 × 30
Built by Richardson, Duck & Co., Stockton-on-Tees.
Renamed *Swindon* 1913
Renamed *Paddington* 1917
21 July 1917 – torpedoed and sunk 250 miles west of Fastnet.

Patagonia 1913 (GRT 6011) 430×55.28×28.8
Built by Craig Taylor & Co., Stockton (Yard No. 154)
Torpedoed 15 September 1915, 10½ miles NE of Odessa.

Penistone 1913 (GRT 4139) 370×40×25.9
Built by Craig Taylor & Co. Ltd. Stockton-on-Tees
11 October 1918 – torpedoed and sunk 145 miles SW by S of Nantucket.

Peterston 1892 (GRT 2768) 321×40×21
Built by Thomas Turnbull, Whitehall Dockyard, Whitby. Daniel Radcliffe received his early training with the Turnbull Brothers who were also shipowners in Cardiff where he was for some time a clerk. Evan Thomas Radcliffe in the early days of the company had their offices at Philip and Lewis Turnbull's premises.
1913 – sold to Artaza & Co., Bilbao named *Arpillao*

Peterston 1925 (GRT 4680) 385.45×52×26
Built by Bartram & Co., South Dock, Sunderland. Cost £84,647
Delivered 23 February 1925
1948 – sold Gowan shipping Co. as *Burhaven*
1950 – sold A.G. Tsauliris as *Andrew T.*
1953 – sold Shamrock Shipping Co. as *Raloo*
1957 – sold to Costa Rica as *Paraporti*
27 July 1959 – scrapped at Antwerp.

Picton 1906 (GRT 5084) 392×52×30
Built by Richardson Duck & Co. Stockton-on-Tees. Cost £48,939
23 May 1927 – sold to Williams & Mordey Ltd., Cardiff for £24,132 as *Seven Seas Transport*
1927 – sold to German owners W. Kunstmann – named *Heinz W Kunstmann*
1937 – renamed *Herta Engelin Fritzen* (same owners)
25 October 1941 – lost of Hook of Holland.

PLM 17 (Managed Vessel) 1922 (GRT 4008) 345×45×27
Built Smiths Dock, Middlesborough for French owners.

Possidon 1909 (GRT 3744) 346.3×50.8×23.1
Built by W. Gray & Co. Ltd., West Hartlepool for Greek owners.
Chartered 1921-1933

Radcliffe Trader 1956 (GRT 622)
ex *Silloth Trader* (1980), ex *Rosemary D.* (1974), ex *Valerie B* (1973), ex *Sarsfield* (1970), ex *Edgefield* (1965), ex *Spolesto* (1956).
Built by Noord Nederlandse Scheepswerven N.V., Groningen. Purchased by E.T.R. from Gillie & Blair Ltd. (Stag Line).

Radcliffe Venturer 1964 (GRT 504)
ex *Bea* (1980), ex *Hattstedt* (1974), ex *Henriette* (1972) ex *Tilly* (1969).
Built by N.V. Bodewes Schps., Martenshoek, Netherlands.
Purchased from Baltic Schooner Association, Cayman Islands June 1980.

Samskern (Managed Vessel) 1944 (GRT 7210) 423 × 59 × 34.8
Built by Bethlehem Fairfield Shipyard, Baltimore.

Sarah Radcliffe 1889 (GRT 1440) 272 × 32.10 × 21′11″
Built by Ropner, Stockton-on-Tees
April 1910 – renamed *Iolo*
May 1914 – Sold to Constantine Hadjipateras of Greece as *Archimedes;* renamed *Olteria* then sold to Romania as *Latium.*
1930 – sold to D.B. Georgiades, Piraeus as *Margarita*
3 June 1952 – Broken up.

Sarah Radcliffe 1910
See *Dunraven* 1896

Senta 1919 (GRT 3785) 340 × 48.2 × 26
Built by Union Ironworks, Alameda, California, USA
Norwegian vessel owned by Skibs A.
Chartered from Ministry of War Transport 1941-45

Stolt Llandaff 1971 (GRT 15,585) 560′1″ × 79′2″ × 34′6¾″
Tanker built by N.V. Boelwerf S.A., Tamise, for Anthony Radcliffe S.S. Co. Ltd.
The company was taken over by the Stolt Corporation and the vessel was leased back to ETR until December 1981.

Swindon 1899 (GRT 3847) 351 × 48 × 28.4
Built by Richardson, Duck & Co., Stockton-on-Tees
Named *Badminton* 1912
1914 – sunk by submarine gunfire 63 miles NE by N of Cape Carbon, Algeria (23 July)

Swindon 1913
See *Patagonia* 1906

Swindon 1917 (GRT 4240) 390 × 53.3 × 23.5
Built by W. Pickersgill & Sons, Sunderland;
1917 – sold to Johnston Line as *Cottesmore*
1920 – sold to D.&T.C. Adams as *Avonmede*
1924 – sold to J.&C. Harrison as *Harpalion*
1931 – sold to N.G. Livanos, Chios as *Theofano*
1937 – sold to V.J. Pateras, Chios as *Dirphys*
8 June 1941 – torpedoed NE of St. Johns, Newfoundland

Torvanger 1920 (GRT 6568) 420.1 × 54.0 × 34.4
Built W. Doxford, Sunderland
Owned by Westfal-hausen & Co. Norway
Chartered from Ministry of War Transport 1942

Varangberg 1915 (GRT 2842) 282.8 × 43.6 × 252
Built Great Lakes Eng. Works, Ashtabula, Oregon, USA
Norwegian vessel owned by A/S Malmfart.
Chartered from Ministry of War Transport 1941-46

Vera Radcliffe 1925 (GRT 5587) 415 × 55.5 × 36.3
Built by Craig, Taylor & Co., Stockton-on-Tees.
Delivered 6 January 1925 for £99,393
June 1944 – sold to government for £75,000. Sunk as blockship on Normandy beaches.

Walter Thomas 1884 (GRT 2213) 296 × 37.4 × 24.5
Named after Captain Evan Thomas's only son Walter Hezekiah Thomas.
Built by Palmers of Jarrow
Sunk 12 July 1901 after collision with *Romney* off Europa Pont, Straits of Gibraltar on a voyage from Penarth to Derindje.

Washington 1907 (GRT 5079) 378 × 52 × 30
Built by Richardson, Duck & Co., Stockton-on-Tees. Cost £52,392
3 May – torpedoed and sunk off Genoa (Rapallo Bay) while on time charter to Italian State Railways.

Wimborne 1898 (GRT 3466) 339 × 46 × 27.3
Built by Richardson, Duck & Co., Stockton-on-Tees for £35,556

On 7 November 1910 she was lost at Tolpedu off Polperro, Cornwall, while on voyage in ballast from Rotterdam to Barry. There were no casualties.

Wimborne 1911 (GRT 6078) 415 × 55 × 28.8
Built by Craig, Taylor & Co., Stockton-on-Tees. Cost £54,011
1936 – sold Halcyon Lign, Rotterdam, named *Stad Schiedam* for £16,006
16 September 1940 – sunk after explosion, believed sabotage 37 °N by 64 °W on voyage from Bermuda to Halifax, Nova Scotia.

Windsor 1897 (GRT 4074) 370 × 46.6 × 27.3
Built by Ropner & Son, Stockton-on-Tees. Delivered 21 July 1897
27 November 1911 – name changed to *Jane Radcliffe*
Torpedoed and sunk 2 miles SW off Antimilo, Greek Archipelago, 28 November 1917.

Windsor 1911 (GRT 6055) 430 × 55.6 × 28.7
Built by Craig, Taylor & Co., Stockton-on-Tees. Delivered December 1911 (Yard No. 148)
Sunk by gunfire from submarine 70 miles SW off Lizard, 21 October 1915.

Windsor 1915
See *Clarissa Radcliffe* 1917

W. I. Radcliffe 1886 (GRT 2076) 280 × 35 × 20
Built Palmers Co., Newcastle.
Sold in 1903 to the Aber-porth S.S. Co. (Dan Jenkins) renamed *Aberporth*
Wrecked.
The Jenkins Bros. were well known Cardiff shipowners with a substantial fleet. One member of the family, Daniel (Bryntirion, Aberporth) broke away from the family group to establish the Aberporth S.S. Co. It was a failure and the firm was soon bankrupt and the ship wrecked.

W.I. Radcliffe 1904 (GRT 4748) 383 × 50.9 × 30.3
Built by Richardson, Duck & Co., Stockton-on-Tees
(Wyndham Ivor Radcliffe was Henry Radcliffe's son)
Renamed *Llancarvan* – 13 March 1917
Torpedoed and sunk 370 miles E by N from San Miguel, Azores, 16 May 1918.

W.I. Radcliffe 1917 (GRT 6042) 430 × 55.6 × 28.7
Built 1913 as *Clarissa Radcliffe* by Craig, Taylor & Co., Stockton-on-Tees,

delivered April 1913 (Yard No. 155)
1917 – renamed *W.I. Radcliffe*
12 March 1918 – torpedoed by submarine in English Channel, but made port.
18 April 1935 – sold to N. Eusthattion & Co., Piraeus, named *Marietta*
1939 – sold to Leonhardt & Blumsey – *Karl Leonhardt*
16 March 1946 – Scuttled with ammunition in Skaggerak.

Wynnstay 1884 (GRT 1541) 209 × 36.4 × 18
Built by Palmers of Jarrow.
Sold in June 1902 for £9500 to L. Overgaard, Norway – *Nora.*

References

1. Edwards, O. M., *Wales*, (1901)
2. ibid.
3. Chappell, E. L., *History of the Port of Cardiff* (Cardiff, 1939) p. 121
4. Jenkins, J. G., 'Herring Fishing in Wales', *Maritime Wales* (Vol. 4 1979) pp. 5 – 32
5. Jenkins, David, 'Aber-porth: A Study of a Coastal Village in South Cardiganshire', *Welsh Rural Communities* (Cardiff 1960), p. 3
6. Prospectus of the Gwenllian Thomas S.S. Co., 1881
7. Dobbin, E. Lloyd, *South Wales as the Chief Industrial Centre of the United Kingdom* (Cardiff n.d.) p. 265
8. *Men of the Period* (London, Biographical Publicity Company, 1898)
9. *Anne Wheaton* (227 tons); *Jessie Anning* (275 tons); *Mary Anning* (169 tons)
10. *Henry Anning* (1075 tons); *Mary Anning* (797 tons): *Richard Anning* (752 tons)
11. Daunton, M. J., *Coal Metropolis Cardiff 1870 – 1914* (Leicester University Press 1977) p. 65
12. Anne Thomas; Anthony Radcliffe; Bala; Douglas Hill; Dunraven; Ethel Radcliffe; Euston; Gwenllian Thomas; Iolo Morgannwg; Jane Radcliffe; Llanberis; Llandudno; Llangorse; Llanover; Manchester; Mary Thomas; Paddington; Sarah Radcliffe; Swindon; W. I. Radcliffe; Walter Thomas; Wimborne; Windsor; Wynnstay
13. Daunton, op. cit., p. 227
14. Chappell, op. cit., p. 121
15. A. H. Jones Personal Correspondence
16. *South Wales Daily News*, 17 December 1921
17. Unpublished MS at Welsh Industrial and Maritime Museum